M000196363

Home Run's
Most Wanted™

Other Sports Titles from Potomac Books

Soccer's Most Wanted II™: The Top 10 Book of More Glorious Goals, Superb Saves, and Fantastic Free-Kicks by Jeff Carlisle

The World Series' Most Wanted™: The Top 10 Book of Championship Teams, Broken Dreams, and October Oddities by John Snyder

Baseball's Most Wanted™: The Top 10 Book of the National Pastime's Outrageous Offenders, Lucky Bounces, and Other Oddities by Floyd Conner

Baseball's Most Wanted™ II: The Top 10 Book of More Bad Hops, Screwball Players, and other Oddities by Floyd Conner

The Year That Changed the Game: The Memorable Months That Shaped Pro Football by Jonathan Rand

Tennis Confidential II: More of Today's Greatest Players, Matches, and Controversies by Paul Fein

Home Run's Most Wanted™

The Top 10 Book of Monumental
Dingers, Prodigious Swingers, and
Everything Long-Ball

David Vincent

Potomac Books, Inc.
WASHINGTON, D.C.

Copyright © 2009 Potomac Books, Inc.

Published in the United States by Potomac Books, Inc. All rights reserved. No part of this book may be reproduced in any manner whatsoever without written permission from the publisher, except in the case of brief quotations embodied in critical articles and reviews.

Library of Congress Cataloging-in-Publication Data

Vincent, David, 1949 July 26-
Home run's most wanted : the top 10 book of monumental dingers, prodigious swingers, and everything long-ball / David Vincent.
p. cm.
Includes index.
ISBN 978-1-59797-192-8 (pbk. : alk. paper)
1. Home runs (Baseball)—United States—History. 2. Home runs (Baseball)—United States—Statistics. I. Title.
GV868.4.V57 2009
796.357'26—dc22
2008055632

Printed in the United States of America on acid-free paper that meets the American National Standards Institute Z39-48 Standard.

Potomac Books, Inc.
22841 Quicksilver Drive
Dulles, Virginia 20166

First Edition

10 9 8 7 6 5 4 3 2 1

Contents

Contents

Illustrations

Introduction

F ans of all sports look for what might be termed the "macho" event. In track, people are fascinated with those athletes who can run the fastest or jump the highest. In football, long passes, long kick returns, and long runs from scrimmage are fan favorites. In baseball, the parallel event is the home run. For decades, baseball enthusiasts have been thrilled to see the big boppers smack a baseball hundreds of feet over a wall to create instant runs. Whether it is Babe Ruth at the start of the Lively Ball Era or Alex Rodriguez at the start of the 21st century, sluggers draw the attention of most fans and writers. In a 1929 *Chicago Tribune* column, Westbrook Pegler wrote: "The home run is just what it takes to make the customers sit up and twitch." Even an international shoe company played on this with a commercial that proclaimed, "Chicks dig the long ball!"

This book of lists takes a sometimes serious and sometimes humorous look at baseball's ultimate weapon. Many of the games best-known sluggers are chronicled here, but we also discuss some of the lesser-known players—in some cases hitters who will not be elected to an All Star team or the Baseball

Hall of Fame but nevertheless have performed a memorable home run feat. We have also included lists that talk about folks who have slugged exactly zero home runs: broadcasters, umpires and players' wives. What are not here are lists such as "Career Home Run Leaders," which can be found in many places in print and online.

There are 61* ten-item lists in the book. In 1961, Roger Maris slugged 61 homers to surpass the single-season record set by Babe Ruth in 1927. The American League had expanded by two teams for that season and also increased the schedule from 154 to 162 games. In July 1961, then-commissioner Ford Frick declared that a batter would have to beat the record in the first 154 games of the season or there would have to be some "distinctive mark" in the record books. This mark has come to be known as "the asterisk," although an asterisk was never applied to the record book. There was a movie titled *61** about that 1961 season, with the title playing on the apocryphal asterisk. Here we only have sixty lists of ten items each and one list (you will have to find it) with only nine items in it—thus the "distinctive mark" each time we talk about 61* lists.

Many of these lists have grown out of questions I have been asked by major league teams and the media covering those teams. The unquestioned leader in this regard is Jayson Stark of ESPN, who continues to come up with crazy twists on everyday events. Among the hundreds of people who have asked thousands of questions through the years, three writers stand out as having asked many consistently interesting queries: Bill Arnold, John Lowe, and Mark Camps. Thanks to these guys and the legion of others who have helped generate ideas that have morphed into this book.

Thanks to my wife, JoLynne, and to my friend, Dave Smith, for their help with this text. Also, thanks to Kevin Cuddihy and Jennifer Waldrop of Potomac Books, Inc., for turning my manuscript into the book you are holding. This book is for my son, Tim, with whom I spent many hours working in a minor league press box—one of the best baseball memories I have.

All numbers are valid through the 2008 season.

Gentlemen, Start Your Swinging

The first chapter of this book has to be a list of firsts. The following gentlemen were the first to perform the feat listed. Being first at something has a certain cachet to it, even though it usually only means you were in the right place at the right time.

1. FIRST HOME RUN IN THE NATIONAL LEAGUE

On May 2, 1876, Ross Barnes of the Chicago White Stockings (now Cubs) hit a home run in the fifth inning of the fourth White Stockings game, which was played at the Avenue Grounds in Cincinnati. This was the first home run in the fledgling National League, which had started play on April 22.

2. FIRST HOME RUN IN THE AMERICAN LEAGUE

Erve Beck of the Cleveland Blues (now Indians) hit the first home run in the history of the American League on April 25, 1901, the second day that the league played. Beck hit a line drive over the right field fence in the second inning of the contest at Chicago's South Side Park. The Blues and White Sox had played the first game in the history of the league the previous day.

3. **FIRST EXTRA INNING HOME RUN**

On June 29, 1876, catcher Pop Snyder of the Louisville Grays hit the first extra inning home run in major league history off Joe Borden of the Boston Red Caps (now the Atlanta Braves). It came in the tenth inning of a game played at Louisville Baseball Park and won the game for the Grays, 8-6. The Louisville franchise only played two years before folding.

4. **FIRST HOME RUN TO LEAD OFF A GAME**

Jack Remsen was the first batter of the game for the Hartford Dark Blues on July 6, 1876, in a game played against the White Stockings in Chicago. He homered off Al Spalding, who later founded a sporting goods company that still exists bearing his name. This was the first time that the first batter of a game for a team hit a four-bagger.

5. **FIRST GRAND SLAM**

Roger Connor, who held the career homer record before Babe Ruth, hit the first grand slam in history on September 10, 1881, while playing for the Troy Trojans. The slam, hit in the ninth inning of a game played in Albany, provided the winning margin for the Trojans, as they beat the Worcester Ruby Legs, 8-7. The salami came at the expense of Lee Richmond, who had thrown the first perfect game in history on June 12, 1880.

6. **FIRST HOME RUN BY A PINCH HITTER**

On May 14, 1892, Tom Daly of the Brooklyn Bridegrooms (now Los Angeles Dodgers) pinch-hit for left fielder Hub Collins. Before this season, such substitutes were not allowed. Daly hit in the top of the ninth inning and slugged the majors' first pinch homer. He remained in the game in the bottom of the frame in left field, as Brooklyn lost to the Boston Beaneaters (now Atlanta Braves), 8-7.

7. FIRST HOME RUN IN THE WORLD SERIES

The first modern World Series was played in 1903 as the Boston Americans (now Red Sox) defeated the Pittsburgh Pirates. In game one, played on October 1, Jimmy Sebring of the Pirates hit the first Series homer off Cy Young. It came in the seventh inning with Pittsburgh already leading, 6-0, in a game they won, 7-3.

8. FIRST HOME RUN IN THE ALL STAR GAME

In 1933, Chicago sportswriter Arch Ward had the idea to play a "Game of the Century" that would feature the best players in the majors. It was meant to be a one-time contest but has become a weeklong series of events in the twenty-first century. In the third inning of that first contest, played on July 6, Babe Ruth hit a two-run homer to put the American League ahead, 3-0, in a game they won, 4-1. This was the Babe's only four-bagger in the Midsummer Classic, as he was near the end of his career in 1933.

9. FIRST HOME RUN IN A NIGHT GAME

The first night game in major league history was played in Cincinnati on May 24, 1935. The Reds played seven night games that season, one against each opponent. On July 10, the opponent was the Brooklyn Dodgers and Reds left fielder Babe Herman hit a solo home run in the seventh inning off Dutch Leonard for the first-ever home run under the lights. The Reds won the contest, 15-2.

10. FIRST HOME RUN BY A DESIGNATED HITTER

In 1973, the American League voted to use a "designated pinch hitter" for the pitcher, thus changing the way the game has been played ever since that time. The first such designated hitter to smack a four-bagger was Tony Oliva of the

Minnesota Twins, who hit a two-run shot in the top of the first inning in Oakland on April 6. The Twins went on to win their first game of the season, 8-3.

The Name Game

Many players have had interesting or colorful nicknames through the years and some of these nicknames relate to home run hitting prowess. The art of creating great nicknames seems to be a dying art, but there are still cool ones occasionally applied to baseball people in the 21st century.

1. THE SULTAN OF SWAT

George Herman "Babe" Ruth had many nicknames during his career but perhaps this is the most famous. Ruth swatted 714 circuit drives in his career and out-homered every other American League team in 1920 when he smacked 54.

2. HOME RUN BAKER

John Franklin Baker hit 96 home runs in his career and never hit more than 12 in one season. These totals are typical of the Deadball Era in which he played, but Baker earned his sobriquet for his two timely four-baggers on consecutive days in the 1911 World Series.

3. THE THUMPER

Theodore Samuel Williams, like Babe Ruth, had many nicknames. Williams hit more home runs than any other Red Sox player in history and was a combat pilot for the U.S. Marine Corps in Korea. Contrary to public belief, he never saw combat during World War II, although he trained as a Marine pilot then.

4. THE RAJAH OF SWAT

Rogers Hornsby's nickname was a play on that of Babe Ruth. Hornsby starred in the National League during the same time that Ruth tore up the American League with his swatting ability. Hornsby slugged 243 homers from 1921 through 1930, second to Ruth for that period and was the first National League player to hit 40 home runs in one season.

5. THE HAMMER

Henry Louis Aaron hit 755 home runs in his 23-year career with at least 20 four-baggers for 20 consecutive seasons. He has also been called "Hammerin' Hank," a name that was also applied to Henry Benjamin Greenberg in the 1930s.

6. KONG KINGMAN

David Arthur Kingman's nickname was a play on both his ability to hit long fly balls and the popular movie ape, King Kong. In 1977, Kingman played and homered in all four divisions in the majors. He hit nine homers for the Mets (NL East), eleven for the Padres (NL West), two for the Angels (AL West), and four for the Yankees (AL East). He is the only batter to accomplish this feat and no one has matched it in the six-division era, which started in 1994.

7. JUAN GONE

Juan Alberto Gonzalez led the American League in homers in 1992 and 1993 and is the career leader for the Rangers. His nickname plays on his last name "Gon" and his ability to make the ball disappear ("gone").

8. SLAMMIN' SAMMY

Samuel Peralta Sosa hit at least 60 homers in three of four seasons from 1998 through 2001 and is the only player to slug 60 three times. Sosa became the fifth player to hit 600 career circuit clouts on June 20, 2007, when he connected off Jason Marquis of the Chicago Cubs, Sosa's former team. Sammy had never homered against the Cubbies until that day!

9. THE BASH BROTHERS

In the late 1980s and early 1990s, two sluggers, Mark David McGwire and Jose Canseco, led the Athletics. They homered in the same game 46 times during their time together in Oakland, thus proving their nickname, which is a play on a popular act that started on television and later made its way to concerts and movies—The Blues Brothers.

10. THE SULTAN OF SWAT STATS

Another play on Babe Ruth's nickname, this one is applied to the author of this book, David Vincent. Jayson Stark of ESPN created it when he was writing for the *Philadelphia Inquirer*, and he continues to use it with the "World-Wide Leader in Sports."

Repeat Trip to the Slammer

Ten American League players have hit two grand slams in one game. Two clubs have cornered the market on this feat, as four of these slammers played for the Boston Red Sox and three for the Baltimore Orioles. By the way, two National Leaguers have also performed this feat, pitcher Tony Cloninger of the Braves in 1966 and Fernando Tatis of the Cardinals in 1999, the latter player having hit both of them in the same inning—off the same pitcher, Chan Ho Park!

1. TONY LAZZERI, YANKEES
The New York Yankees second baseman hit two grand slam home runs in one game in Philadelphia on May 24, 1936. No other batter had ever socked two home runs with the bases full in a game before Lazzeri, who hit another homer to lead off the seventh inning in the same contest. He almost hit a fourth home run in the eighth inning but settled for a two-run triple as the ball stayed in the park.

2. JIM TABOR, RED SOX
Jim Tabor of the Red Sox hit four home runs in a holiday doubleheader at Philadelphia on July 4, 1939, with two of the three in the nightcap coming with the bases loaded. This

was the second time a batter had smashed two grand slams in one contest and both came at the expense of the hapless Athletics at Shibe Park in Philadelphia. The BoSox, led by third baseman Tabor, swept the twin bill, 17-7 and 18-12, by hitting seven homers in the two games.

3. **RUDY YORK, RED SOX**

For the third time in history, a player slugged two grand slams in the same game on July 27, 1946, when first baseman Rudy York of the Red Sox performed the feat in St. Louis. Both shots came off Tex Shirley as the Sox beat the Browns, 13-6, on the way to the American League championship.

4. **JIM GENTILE, ORIOLES**

First baseman Jim Gentile of the Baltimore Orioles hit two grand slams in one game on May 9, 1961, at Metropolitan Stadium in Minneapolis. Gentile became the fourth player to perform the feat, all of whom did it in the American League on the road. Gentile's slams came in the first and second innings of the contest, making him the first to hit the blasts in consecutive innings and in consecutive at bats, as he led the Orioles to a 13-5 victory.

5. **JIM NORTHRUP, TIGERS**

On June 24, 1968, Jim Northrup, an outfielder for the Detroit Tigers, hit two grand slams in the same game off the Cleveland Indians, becoming the fifth American Leaguer to accomplish this. Northrup's blasts came in the fifth and sixth innings and only Jim Gentile had hit two slams in consecutive innings before Northrup. Northrup continued the pattern of all two-slam batters as he slugged his on the road.

6. FRAΠK ROBIΠSOΠ, ORIOLES
On June 26, 1970, at Robert F. Kennedy Memorial Stadium in Washington, D.C., outfielder Frank Robinson of the Baltimore Orioles slugged two grand slams in one game. The clouts came in consecutive innings, the fifth and sixth, and propelled the Orioles to a 12-2 victory. Robinson became the sixth AL batter to perform this feat, all of whom had done it on the road. His slams were the last hit at RFK Stadium until August 2005, as the stadium did not host baseball from 1972 through 2004.

7. ROBIΠ VEΠTURA, WHITE SOX
In 1995, third baseman Robin Ventura of the Chicago White Sox hit two of his 18 career grand slams—and they both came in the same game. On September 4, the left-handed swinging Ventura hit his first slam in the fourth inning off lefty Dennis Cook of the Rangers at The Ballpark in Arlington. In the fifth inning, Ventura hit his second slam in as many at bats off right-hander Danny Darwin, as the Pale Hose romped, 14-3. It had been 25 years since a batter had hit two grand slams in the same game.

8. CHRIS HOILES, ORIOLES
On August 14, 1998, catcher Chris Hoiles of the Baltimore Orioles hit two grand slams in one game at Cleveland's Jacobs Field. Hoiles continued the pattern of all previous double-slammers by hitting his shots on the road as he smacked the two four-baggers in the third and eighth innings. The Birds beat the Tribe, 15-3.

q. ΠOMAR GARCIAPARRA, RED SOX
On May 10, 1999, Red Sox shortstop Nomar Garciaparra hit three homers in the game, with a grand slam in the first inning and one in the eighth inning, to become the first player

with two slams to perform the feat in his own ballpark. Boston whipped the Mariners, 12-4, at Boston's historic Fenway Park.

10. BILL MUELLER, RED SOX

Bill Mueller, third baseman for the Boston Red Sox, hit three home runs in one game, including two grand slams in consecutive innings on July 29, 2003. Mueller hit one slam right-handed and one left-handed to become the only player to accomplish that feat. The Sox beat the Rangers in Arlington, 14-7.

Nomar Garciaparra at the plate doing his "toe-tapping" routine before the pitch. *National Baseball Hall of Fame Library/Rich Pilling/MLB Photos*

Hey, Ump!—Game 1

Many players have seen apparent four-baggers turn into something else due to a ruling by an umpire. Some of these have been mistakes by the arbiter, but many are correct calls that nullified the play. Here are some of the best in chronological order.

1. CY WILLIAMS, CUBS
On July 13, 1915, in a game at the Polo Grounds in New York, Cy Williams of the Cubs hit what appeared to be a two-run inside-the-park home run to right-center in the top of the fourth inning. However, Williams missed third base and was called out by umpire Mal Eason. Cubs skipper Roger Bresnahan was ejected by umpire Lord Byron for arguing the call on Williams. The Cubs beat the Giants anyway, 8-4.

2. ALFRED "GREASY" NEALE, REDS
In the second game of a doubleheader on July 12, 1917, at New York's Polo Grounds, Reds left fielder Greasy Neale hit an inside-the-park homer with Hal Chase on base. However, base umpire Pete Harrison had called time before the pitch because of a ball that was loose on the field. Thus, the four-bagger was nullified, but the Reds beat the Giants, 5-1.

3. FRANK SIGAFOOS, TIGERS
On April 21, 1929, Frank Sigafoos hit a ball into the stands for Detroit in St. Louis. However, an umpire had called a balk on the pitch and the home run was wiped out. Detroit won the game, 16-9. Sigafoos finished his career with no home runs in 134 at bats.

4. BABE RUTH, YANKEES (TWICE!)
Babe Ruth hit a ball into the right-centerfield stands at Shibe Park, Philadelphia on April 15, 1930. It struck a loudspeaker horn and bounced back into the playing field. The umpires ruled it a double. The drive came off Lefty Grove in the third inning with one man on base. Later that season, on September 9 off Cy Perkins, Ruth repeated his April drive into the right-centerfield stands in Philadelphia. This also hit the speaker and returned to the field and was once again ruled in play by the umpires.

5. MICKEY MANTLE, YANKEES
On April 28, 1956, Mickey Mantle drilled a ball into the Fenway Park center field bleachers in the eighth inning. The blast off Dave Sisler landed three or four rows up in the stands. The ball bounced once while a number of fans tried to grab it and then bounced back onto the field. Mantle hustled and beat the throw to third base. Second base umpire Eddie Rommel ruled that the ball hit the top of the wall and did not go into the stands. Manager Casey Stengel, coaches Bill Dickey and Frank Crosetti, and catcher Yogi Berra surrounded Rommel, trying to convince him that his ruling was incorrect. The argument took five minutes and Rommel ejected Stengel.

6. HARMON KILLEBREW, SENATORS
According to fellow 500-homer slugger Ted Williams, Harmon Killebrew was robbed of a home run on July 1, 1959, in the

bottom of the seventh inning. The Killer blasted a Jerry Casale pitch toward left field where Williams was patrolling. According to umpire Bob Stewart, the ball struck the visiting bullpen fence at Griffith Stadium and was not out of the park. The ball rolled almost all the way back to third base. Williams stood watching the ball roll with his hands on his hips. By Williams' account, the ball struck the screen on the left field pole a couple of feet above the fence. "I saw no point in chasing a home run." Killebrew was awarded a double on the play.

7. **BROOKS ROBINSON, ORIOLES**
On August 2, 1964, in Kansas City, Brooks Robinson hit a ball down the line that struck the left field pole high above the fence. Umpire John Rice ruled it in play and Robinson was tagged out sliding into third base. Rice admitted after the game that he probably made a mistake.

8. **RON SWOBODA, METS**
Ron Swoboda lost a grand slam at Crosley Field in Cincinnati on April 30, 1965. In the first inning, after a single, double, and intentional walk, Swoboda hit a long drive to center field off John Tsitouris. At that time, there was a double fence; the main wall was concrete and it was topped with a plywood extension to protect the road construction crew outside. The concrete was in play while the plywood was a homer; Swoboda's ball hit the plywood and bounced back. Vada Pinson threw the ball back to the infield and second base umpire Frank Secory ruled that the ball was in play. The slam turned into an RBI single. Coach Yogi Berra was ejected for the first time in his National League career for arguing the call. After the game he uttered one of his classic lines: "Anyone who can't hear the difference between wood and concrete must be blind."

9. HANK AARON, BRAVES

On August 18, 1965, Hank Aaron of Milwaukee hit a Curt
Simmons pitch onto the pavilion roof at Busch Stadium in St.
Louis for an apparent homer. However, umpire Chris
Pelekoudas called Aaron out for being out of the batter's box
when he connected. At the time, Aaron had 393 homers on
his way to 755 in his career.

10. STEVE BUSBY, ROYALS

In the first inning of a game in Anaheim on September 20,
1972, Kansas City pitcher Steve Busby hit a grand slam homer
off Lloyd Allen. Unfortunately, first base umpire John Rice
called time as the play started, which nullified the blast. John
Mayberry had already hit a slam in the inning so the Royals
would have been added to the very short list of teams with
two grand slams in one inning had the play stood.

Hey, Ump!—
Let's Play Two!

This list is a continuation of the chronological list of calls that wiped out home runs.

1. TED SIMMONS, CARDINALS

On July 21, 1975, catcher Ted Simmons hit a homer to lead off the fourth inning in San Diego. However, Padres manager John McNamara claimed that his bat was illegal. Home plate umpire Art Williams agreed with McNamara because there were grooves cut into the fat part of the bat, clearly further than the 18" limit from the handle. Williams ruled Simmons out and the bat was confiscated by crew chief Ed Vargo. The Cardinals protested the game, but then they won 4-0, thus making the protest moot.

2. DON MONEY, BREWERS

On the second day of the 1976 season in Milwaukee, Don Money batted with the bases loaded in the bottom of the ninth inning and the Brewers behind the Yankees, 9-6. Before Dave Pagan delivered his second pitch to Money, New York manager Billy Martin yelled to first baseman Chris Chambliss to call time. Chambliss asked umpire Jim McKean. Money hit the pitch and circled the bases. The Brewers celebrated and

21

went into the clubhouse thinking they had won for the second time in two games. However, before Money crossed the plate Martin was on the field arguing with McKean. After a couple of minutes of Martin's tirade, the umpires sent for the Brewers to come back on the field. The Brewers were obviously upset about the call. First base coach Harvey Kuenn said that the pitcher was already in his motion when Chambliss yelled for time. Some Brewers went so far as to say that Martin intimidated McKean into reversing the homer. The Yankees won the game, 9-7, and the Brewers protested the outcome to no avail.

3. BUTCH HOBSON, RED SOX
During the 1977 season, BoSox third baseman Butch Hobson lost two homers to umpire calls at Fenway Park. On May 28, Hobson lost a homer off Marty Pattin because of a ruling by umpire Terry Cooney. Hobson's seventh inning hit went into the screen over Fenway Park's left field wall. Unfortunately, it bounced off a light tower and came back onto the field and was ruled in play. Hobson received credit for an RBI double. Then, on July 21 in the seventh inning of game one, Hobson hit a ball into the center field stands that was ruled off the wall and in play by Ted Hendry. The Red Sox claimed that the ball caromed off a fan and back onto the field, but Hobson ended up with a double off Wayne Garland. Hobson batted a second time in the inning, and homered, and thus would have joined the short list of players with two home runs in one inning were it not for the call on the first at bat.

4. JOHN LOWENSTEIN, RANGERS
On September 6, 1978, in the top of the third inning in Anaheim, umpire Bill Deegan called time when a paper airplane landed on the field. Angels hurler Paul Hartzel delivered his

pitch just after the arbiter's call and John Lowenstein hit the ball over the right field fence for an apparent home run. However, due to Deegan's time out call, Lowenstein lost his homer He later walked and scored in the inning—all because of a paper airplane.

5. CARLTON FISK, WHITE SOX

In the bottom of the fifth inning at Comiskey Park on August 14, 1983, Carlton Fisk hit a ball to left field that third base umpire Greg Kosc ruled a home run. However, plate umpire Jim Evans over-ruled Kosc, calling the play fan interference and a double for Fisk. The White Sox lost two runs and manager Tony LaRussa, who was ejected, protested the game. Neither runner scored in the inning and the Orioles won the contest, 2-1.

6. MIKE EASLER, RED SOX

On September 5, 1985, in the first game of a twi-night doubleheader, Boston's Mike Easler lost what would have been his third grand slam in five days. The ball was hit off Cleveland's Neal Heaton in the third inning and hit the light tower above Fenway Park's fabled left field wall. Umpire Ted Hendry, part of a three-man crew, ruled it in play. Indians' left fielder Joe Carter said that the ball clearly left the yard, but Easler ended with a double and three RBIs.

7. RYNE SANDBERG, CUBS

In the bottom of the third inning at Wrigley Field on May 28, 1990, Ryne Sandberg hit a two-run home run just inside the left field pole that third base umpire Bill Hohn ruled a fair ball. However, Giants manager Roger Craig came out and argued the call. After a discussion by the umpires, crew chief (and first base arbiter) Harry Wendelstedt overruled Hohn and called it a foul ball. Television replays clearly showed it to be a fair ball and a homer. Cubs manager Don Zimmer was ejected because of the changed call. Sandberg singled but the Cubs did not score in the frame. However, they won the game, 5-1.

8. SCOTT HATTEBERG, RED SOX
On April 15, 1997, Scott Hatteberg of the Red Sox hit his first major league home run at Fenway Park but lost it to an umpire's call. John Shulock ruled the ball in play and Hatteberg only got to second base on the play. The hit came off Don Wengert of Oakland in the sixth inning and hit a TV camera in center field. (Two batters later, Nomar Garciaparra hit a ball that was ruled a homer even though a fan seemed to reach over the right field wall, touching the ball while it was still in play.)

9. DAVID MCCARTY, RED SOX
At Tropicana Field in St. Petersburg on September 27, 2003, the Boston Red Sox were behind by one run in the top of the ninth inning. Left fielder David McCarty hit a home run into the left field stands. Umpire Joe West ruled fan interference and called him out on it, saying that Tampa Bay's left fielder Carl Crawford could have made the catch. Replays clearly showed it was a home run at least two feet into the stands. That would have tied the score but the Sox lost 5-4.

10. CHASE UTLEY, PHILLIES
On September 26, 2006, at RFK Stadium in Washington, D.C. Chase Utley hit a ball down the right field line that struck the pole for an apparent three-run homer. However, it was ruled a foul ball by first base umpire Rob Drake and no one from the Phillies protested the call. Utley popped out and the Nationals won the game, 4-3.

The Luke Skywalker Club

In recent years, many pundits have referred to the New York Yankees as "The Evil Empire." New York is known as the "Empire State" and the Yankees have been successful for a long time, sometimes crushing their opponents in a similar fashion to the Empire in the *Star Wars* films. This list of sluggers has shown a lot of success against the Evil Empire by hitting more home runs against the Yankees than anyone else in history. The only eligible player not in the Hall of Fame is Rocky Colavito.

1. JIMMIE FOXX

"The Beast" hit 70 home runs in his career against the Yankees. Foxx played for the Philadelphia Athletics and the Boston Red Sox, hitting 524 four-baggers, before finishing his career in the National League with ten more long balls. Foxx hit more four-baggers against the Yankees than any other player in history.

2. TED WILLIAMS

"The Kid" played his entire career with the Boston Red Sox, hitting 62 of his 521 home runs against the Yankees. Of that total, 30 came at Yankee Stadium, known as "The House that Ruth Built," the third highest total at the stadium by a visitor.

3. MANNY RAMIREZ
Ramirez has played for two American League teams, the Indians and the Red Sox, and thus has had plenty of opportunity to smack a big fly against the Yankees. Through the 2008 season, Manny has hit 55 homers against the Yankees, with 29 of them at Yankee Stadium.

4. HANK GREENBERG
Greenberg played for the Tigers for many years before finishing his career with one season in the National League with the Pirates. During his career, he hit 331 major league home runs. Of Greenberg's 306 homers in the American League, 53 came at the expense of Yankee hurlers.

5. CARL YASTRZEMSKI
Just behind Greenberg on the list is another Red Sox Hall of Famer, Carl Yastrzemski. "The Captain" hit 52 homers against the Yankees out of his 452 career circuit drives.

6. HARMON KILLEBREW
"The Killer" hit 573 home runs for two teams in his 22-year career with 47 of them against the Yankees. The Idaho native led the American League in homers six times, including three consecutive years starting in 1962. He hit at least 40 home runs in eight seasons, including four in a row from 1961 through 1964, topping out at 49, and he had six consecutive years with 30.

7. RAFAEL PALMEIRO
Palmeiro slugged 569 homers for three teams, two in the American and one in the National League, with 47 of them

against the Yankees. Raffy never led his league in any one season and has the most career homers for a batter who never was a league leader. He hit more than 200 homers for each of two teams, with 321 for the Rangers and 223 for the Baltimore Orioles, one of five batters to accomplish this.

8. GOOSE GOSLIN

Leon Allen Goslin hit 46 four-baggers against the Yankees and holds the record for most homers at Yankee Stadium by an opponent with 32. Goslin is the only player on this list who did not hit at least 300 home runs, as he finished with 248 while playing for three different squads.

9. AL SIMMONS

Simmons hit 27 homers at Yankee Stadium and 45 against the Yankees in his long career. He smacked 307 home runs for five American and two National League teams.

10. ROCKY COLAVITO

New York City native Rocky Colavito clouted 44 of his 374 career home runs against the team from the Bronx. He is the only slugger on the list who also played for the Yankees, as he ended his career there, slugging five for the Empire.

Working Overtime

The longest major league game in terms of innings occurred on May 1, 1920, at Braves Field in Boston, where
the Brooklyn Robins (now Los Angeles Dodgers) and Boston (now Atlanta) Braves played a 26-inning, 1-1 tie with no
batter hitting a home run. The game was stopped due to dark-
ness, as this was before lights existed on playing fields. Larry
Doyle of the New York (now San Francisco) Giants was the
first batter to homer in the 20th inning, or later, of a game
when he hit an inside-the-park homer off Babe Adams of the
Pirates, at Forbes Field in Pittsburgh. Doyle's two-run clout in
the 21st inning on July 17, 1914, provided the winning margin as the Giants won the contest, 3-1. Here are the other ten
instances of a batter smacking a four-bagger in the 20th inning or later, presented in chronological order.

1. JACK REED, 22
It took 48 years for someone to replicate Larry Doyle's feat.
The Yankees played a 22-inning game at Tiger Stadium on
June 24, 1962, and Jack Reed, the third right fielder of the
day for New York, hit the only home run of his career in the
top of the 22nd frame, as the Yankees beat the Tigers, 9-7.

The homer drove in Roger Maris, who had walked before Reed batted.

2. KEN MCMULLEN, 20

On August 9, 1967, the Washington Senators played at Metropolitan Stadium in Minneapolis. The game was decided in the top of the 20th inning when Ken McMullen hit a solo homer to lead off the frame. The Senators later scored another run, as they beat the Twins, 9-7.

3 AND 4. JOE LAHOUD AND TOMMY HARPER, 20

The Boston Red Sox invaded Sick's Stadium in Seattle on July 27, 1969, to play the Pilots. Each team scored a single run in the first nine innings and they each added a tally in the 19th frame. In the top of the 20th inning, the Red Sox scored two runs on a Joe Lahoud home run and added another in the inning. In the bottom of the inning, with two out, Tommy Harper hit a solo homer, but the run was not enough, as Boston won, 5-3. Before this day, only three batters had homered as late as the 20th inning in 93 years and yet two players performed the feat in the same game.

5. DICK ALLEN, 21

The Indians and White Sox played 16 innings at Chicago's Comiskey Park on May 26, 1973, before the game was suspended because of a curfew, with the teams tied, 2-2. The contest was resumed two days later, and the Indians scored one run in the top of the 21st inning. The White Sox quickly scored a run to tie the game in the bottom of the frame. Then with two out and two runners on base, Dick Allen hit a game-ending four-bagger as the White Sox won, 6-3. All statistics from the resumed portion of the game count as if they had happened on the original day, thus Allen's bomb is listed as May 26, even though he hit it about 48 hours later!

6. MERV RETTENMUND, 21

On May 21, 1977, in the 19th game played at the newly opened Olympic Stadium in Montreal, the Padres played a 21-inning contest with the host Expos. Merv Rettenmund's three-run shot in the top of the 21st provided the winning margin for the Padres, as they won the contest, 11-8. Incredibly, the Expos scored only eight runs while collecting 25 hits and eight walks in the game.

7 AND 8. BEN OGLIVIE, 21, AND HAROLD BAINES, 25

For the second time in 11 years, a game was suspended at Chicago's Comiskey Park that featured late home runs. On May 8, 1984, the Brewers were playing the White Sox and the game was stopped after the 17th inning with the score tied, 3-3. Both teams had scored twice in the 9th inning to keep the game going. The contest was resumed the next day and Brewers left fielder Ben Oglivie hit a three-run homer in the top of the 21st inning. However, the Sox scored three in the bottom of the inning without benefit of a four-bagger. The teams played three more scoreless innings before Harold Baines ended the contest with a solo-homer on the 753rd pitch of the battle. This clout by Baines is the latest inning for a home run in history. With only 11 home runs in the 20th inning or later, it is hard to believe that there are two instances of two in the same game.

9. RICK DEMPSEY, 22

On August 23, 1989, the Dodgers and Expos battled for 22 innings at Olympic Stadium in Montreal. In the bottom of the eighth inning, Rick Dempsey entered the game as the Dodger catcher and caught the rest of the game. In the 22nd inning, Dempsey led off against his former battery-mate with the Baltimore Orioles, Dennis Martinez, and homered for the only run of the game. This is the latest inning in history for a home run that provided all the runs of a game. When Dempsey was asked years later if the many times he caught Martinez helped him know what pitch to expect, he laughed and admitted that it did.

10. **PEDRO MUNOZ, 22**

On August 31, 1993, Pedro Munoz of the Minnesota Twins, who had entered the contest as a pinch hitter in the 20th inning, led off the bottom of the 22nd inning at the Metrodome with a game-ending solo homer to right-center field. This is the only instance of a late homer hit indoors and (surprisingly) only the third game-ending blast on the list.

Don't Unpack That Suitcase

M any players have had long, productive careers while playing for only one team. At the other end of that spectrum is Todd Zeile, who, while a productive major leaguer,
played and homered for 11 different clubs, totaling 253 four-
baggers in his career. Zeile, a third baseman, hit home runs
for more major league teams than anyone else in history. He
started his major league career with the St. Louis Cardinals,
for whom he played from 1989 through June 15, 1995, hitting 75 four-baggers. Here are the other ten teams for whom
Zeile homered.

1. CHICAGO CUBS
Zeile was traded to the Cubs on June 16, 1995, and played
79 games through the end of that season. He smacked nine
home runs for the Cubs in that partial season with the Wrigley
residents.

2. PHILADELPHIA PHILLIES
After the 1995 season, Zeile became a free agent and signed
with the Phillies, for whom he played 134 games in 1996. He
slugged 20 home runs before being traded to the Baltimore
Orioles on August 29, 1996.

3. **BALTIMORE ORIOLES**

Zeile finished the 1996 season with the Orioles, playing 29 games and hitting five home runs with his first American League squad, and was in the lineup on September 6, when Eddie Murray hit his 500th career homer as an Oriole. At the end of the 1996 season, Zeile again became a free agent.

4. **LOS ANGELES DODGERS**

The Van Nuys, California, native signed with the Los Angeles Dodgers for the 1997 season and, for the first time since 1994, played an entire season with one ball club. Before being traded to the Florida Marlins on May 14, 1998, Zeile hit 38 home runs for the Dodgers.

5. **FLORIDA MARLINS**

After joining the Marlins, Zeile clouted six home runs in 66 games but on July 31, 1998, he was traded for the second time that season. Zeile headed west again, this time to Texas.

6. **TEXAS RANGERS**

Zeile finished the 1998 season and played the entire 1999 season with the Rangers. He hit 30 four-baggers in 208 games with Texas over the one and a half year span. At the end of the 1999 season, Zeile became a free agent for the third time in his career and signed with the New York Mets.

7. **NEW YORK METS**

For the first time since 1993–94, Zeile played two complete seasons with one club, as he played 304 games as a first baseman and hit 32 home runs for the Mets. In 2000, the team played in the World Series and Zeile played in all five games without homering.

8. **COLORADO ROCKIES**

The Mets traded Zeile to the Rockies on January 21, 2002, as part of a three-team, eleven-player deal. Back at third base, Zeile hit 18 home runs for Colorado during the 2002 season.

9. **NEW YORK YANKEES**

Granted free agency after the 2002 season, Zeile signed with the Yankees, for whom he played 66 games in 2003. He homered six times for the Yankees before being released on August 18.

10. **MONTREAL EXPOS**

Two days after being released by the Yankees, Zeile signed with the Montreal Expos (now the Washington Nationals). He finished the season with Montreal, playing in 34 games and hitting five home runs. He became a free agent after the season and joined the New York Mets for a second time and hit his last nine homers, including his only career pinch-hit home run, for the Mets in 2004.

The Avis Awards

The Avis Rent-A-Car company once ran an ad campaign that talked about how they were only Number Two in the car rental business so they worked harder. This list of sluggers hit at least 50 homers in one season and did not lead the league while doing it.

1. SAMMY SOSA, 66

In 1998, Sammy Sosa was the runner-up in one of the greatest home run races of all time. Slammin' Sammy ended the season with 66 big flies but watched Mark McGwire hit 70 that summer to lead the National League and set a new single-season record. Sosa's total also eclipsed the mark set by Roger Maris in 1961, but Sosa accomplished this after McGwire and thus never held the record.

2. SAMMY SOSA, 64

Three years later, Sosa slammed 64 homers in the same season that Barry Bonds broke McGwire's record by hitting 73 long balls. Thus, for the second time, Sosa hit more than 60 long balls in a year in which another slugger broke the single-season record and thus Sosa finished second again while hitting 60 homers.

3. **SAMMY SOSA, 63**

Incredibly, Sosa hit over 60 home runs in one season three times in four years and all three times placed second in the National League. His 63 dingers in 1999 placed him second to Mark McGwire for the second consecutive year as Big Mac stroked 65 that season. Sosa is the only player in history to hit 60 home runs in three seasons and yet he never led his league in any of those campaigns.

4. **MARK MCGWIRE, 58**

Mark McGwire started the 1997 season with the Athletics in the American League. He slugged 34 homers before being traded to the National League Cardinals on July 31. After the trade, McGwire hit 24 more four-baggers in the NL for a season total of 58, the most in the majors that year. However, Ken Griffey, Jr. hit 56 home runs to lead the American League and Larry Walker hit 49 to lead the National League that year, thus McGwire, although he led the majors in 1997, did not lead either league because of the inter-league trade in mid-season. This is the only time a batter has led the majors and not either league.

5. **LUIS GONZALEZ, 57**

In 2001, when Barry Bonds hit 73 home runs and Sammy Sosa hit 64, Luis Gonzalez clouted 57 homers and only placed third in the National League (THIRD WITH 57!). This was his career high for one season, as he never hit more than 31 in any other campaign.

6. **MICKEY MANTLE, 54**

Before 1997, Mickey Mantle held the record for most homers in a season without winning the league title. In 1961, Mantle hit 54 home runs to place second behind teammate Roger

Maris, who broke Babe Ruth's single-season record by hitting 61 four-baggers. Maris and Mantle captured the attention of the baseball world that summer with their chase to the Babe's mark but Mantle fell behind as he spent some of September in the hospital.

7. JIM THOME, 52

Jim Thome hit the most home runs of any season of his career in 2002 when he clouted 52 four-baggers. Unfortunately for Thome, fellow American League star Alex Rodriguez smacked 57 big flies that season to lead the circuit. Thome had just missed the 50 plateau in 2001 when he slugged 49 four-baggers and finished second to ARod's 52 that season.

Jim Thome connects on June 2, 2002, while playing for the Cleveland Indians. *Greg Drezdzon/Cleveland Indians*

8. JIMMIE FOXX, 50

Jimmie Foxx hit at least 50 homers twice in his career. In 1938, Foxx hit exactly 50 but placed second in the Junior Circuit to Hank Greenberg, who smacked 58 dingers that season. Foxx and Greenberg became the first pair of sluggers to each hit at least 50 in the same season in 1938, a feat that has been accomplished many times since then.

9. BRADY ANDERSON, 50

Brady Anderson finished second to Mark McGwire in the 1996 American League home run race when Anderson hit 50 and McGwire 52. It was Anderson's career high and the first of four seasons in which McGwire hit over 50 dingers. Anderson never hit more than 24 in any other year.

10. GREG VAUGHN, 50

Greg Vaughn's 50 season came in 1998 in the National League when Mark McGwire hit 70 and Sammy Sosa hit 66. Thus Vaughn became the first slugger to hit 50 homers and finish third in his league, a feat only Luis Gonzalez has repeated since then.

He's not Heavy, He's My Brother

M any families have had brothers play in the major leagues, often at the same time. Some of these siblings have been teammates but more often face off against each other on the diamond. Here are the only times when two brothers have homered in the same game as opponents.

1. RICK AND WES FERRELL
These North Carolina natives each played in the majors for multiple teams, including some time as teammates. On July 19, 1933, the Indians were in Boston to play the Red Sox. Wes Ferrell, the starting hurler for the Tribe, hit a two-run homer in the top of the fourth inning to extend the team's lead to 5-0. In the bottom of the frame, Boston catcher Rick Ferrell hit his own two-run dinger—off Wes! The Indians won the contest, 8-7, in 13 innings. This is the only instance on this list in which the siblings homered in the same inning.

2. AL AND TONY CUCCINELLO
The Cuccinellos from New York had radically different major league careers. Tony played for 15 years, while Al only played 54 games in 1935. On July 5, 1935, the Brooklyn Dodgers played the Giants at New York's Polo Grounds. Dodger second

baseman Tony Cuccinello hit a solo shot to lead off the top of the eighth inning. Al Cuccinello, a late-inning substitute at third base for the Giants, drove in two runs with his own four-bagger. This was the second of four career homers for Al. The Dodgers routed the Giants in the game, 14-4.

3. DOM AND JOE DIMAGGIO

The DiMaggio family from Northern California was fortunate enough to send three brothers to the big leagues. While the oldest, Vince, played in the National League, Dom played his entire career for the Red Sox and Joe his entire career with the Yankees. In nine seasons, Dominic and Joe saw each other in the opposing dugout many times, but they only hit home runs in the same game one time. On June 30, 1950, the teams played a day/night doubleheader at Fenway Park in Boston. In the evening contest, won by the Sox, 10-2, Dom started the bottom of the sixth inning with a home run and then Joe hit his solo shot in the eighth. The teams combined for six home runs in the two games.

4. CLETE AND KEN BOYER

The Boyers were another family that sent three sons to the big leagues. Cloyd pitched a few years in the early 1950s, while both Clete and Ken played third base. Ken's Cardinals defeated Clete's Yankees in the 1964 World Series. In game seven, played in St. Louis, both brothers hit solo home runs. Ken whacked his in the seventh inning, while Clete smashed his in the top of the ninth. The Boyers are the only brothers to hit home runs in the same World Series game, whether as teammates or opponents.

5. GRAIG AND JIM NETTLES

Graig and Jim Nettles, who were born in San Diego, had two different types of careers in the big leagues. Jim, an outfielder, played 240 games and hit 16 homers, while Graig, a third baseman, played 2,700 games and hit 390 home runs. On June 11, 1972, Jim hit a solo home run for the Twins in Cleveland in the top of the sixth inning. Graig hit his own home run in the bottom of the seventh. The Twins won, 5-3, behind the pitching of Jim Kaat, who also hit a home run to help his cause.

6. GRAIG AND JIM NETTLES

Jim Nettles hit only 16 major league home runs but two of them came in games in which his brother also homered. That's pretty long odds! On September 14, 1974, Graig, now play- ing for the Yankees, hit a home run in the first inning at Tiger Stadium in Detroit as part of a four-run inning. Not to be outdone by his older brother, Jim smacked a four-bagger in the second inning, but his efforts were not enough. The Yan- kees beat the Tigers, 10-7. The Nettles make the list twice and each played for different teams for the two instances.

7. HECTOR AND JOSE CRUZ

Jose, Tommy, and Hector Cruz are natives of Puerto Rico. Tommy played briefly in the majors, but Hector and Jose each enjoyed longer careers. On May 4, 1981, the Astros beat the Cubs at Wrigley Field, 5-4. Jose Cruz gave the Astros a lead in the first inning with his three-run homer. Hector provided the first run of the day for the Cubs with his homer in the sixth frame.

8. AARON AND BRET BOONE

Aaron and Bret Boone, third generation players from the San Diego area, both played infield positions. On September 1, 1999, older brother Bret, a second baseman, hit a two-run home run in the top of the third inning to give the Braves a

2-1 lead. Aaron, a third baseman, hit a homer in the bottom of the eighth, but it was not enough, as the Braves beat the Reds, 8-7, in Cincinnati.

9. AARON AND BRET BOONE

On May 11, 2000, the Boones became the second pair of brothers to make this list twice. Bret, now with the Padres, hit two two-run bombs in the game, one in the first and one in the sixth inning. However, Aaron had the last word that day as he hit a two-run home run in the bottom of the ninth inning to win the game, 11-9, for his team.

10. CESAR AND FELIPE CRESPO

Cesar and Felipe Crespo, from Rio Piedras, Puerto Rico, each had a brief career in the major leagues. Older brother Felipe hit 10 home runs in 262 games, while Cesar hit four in 132 games. On June 7, 2001, Cesar and the Padres visited Felipe and the Giants in San Francisco. While Felipe hit two home runs in the game, his eighth and ninth career four-baggers, Cesar hit one in a winning cause, as the Pads beat the Giants, 10-7.

The Inner Circle

Traditionally, players up the middle of the field (catcher, shortstop, second baseman, and center fielder) have been considered defensive-minded, rather than offensive-minded, players. The players down each line (first and third basemen, left and right fielders) have always been considered the power hitters on a team. These attitudes have been changing in the last few years and sometimes the double play combination around second base can smack a few home runs. Here are ten instances where a team hit exactly four home runs in a game—one by each infielder.

1. DETROIT TIGERS

On August 29, 1943, the Detroit Tigers won the first game of a doubleheader in St. Louis against the Browns, 15-5. The Tigers hit four home runs in the contest, providing eight of their 15 runs in the game. The slugging infield that day consisted of shortstop Joe Hoover, who hit a two-run homer in the third, third baseman Pinky Higgins, who hit a solo drive in the second, first sacker Rudy York, who smacked a two-run clout in the sixth, and second baseman Joe Wood, who hit a three-run homer in the eighth inning. This was Wood's only career home run.

2. **MILWAUKEE BRAVES**

On June 4, 1955, the Milwaukee Braves beat the Philadelphia Phillies, 11-3, at Connie Mack Stadium in the City of
Brotherly Love. Five of the Braves runs in the game scored
on homers. The sluggers that day were shortstop Johnny
Logan (solo homer in the first), third baseman Eddie Mathews
(two-run home run in the third), and back-to-back solo homers in the sixth by first baseman Joe Adcock and second
baseman Danny O'Connell.

3. **CHICAGO CUBS**

In a doubleheader played on September 9, 1955, at Wrigley
Field in Chicago, the Brooklyn Dodgers and the Cubs hit 13
home runs as they split the twin bill. In game two, the Cubs hit
four and lost, 16-9. Third baseman Randy Jackson hit a two-
run clout in the seventh. In the eighth, first baseman Dee Fondy
and second baseman Gene Baker hit back-to-back solo homers and, one out later, shortstop Ernie Banks followed with
his own solo home run.

4. **MILWAUKEE BRAVES (AGAIN!)**

This feat has been performed only ten times in history and
the Braves did it twice in six years. On September 19, 1961,
they lost, 11-10, at Candlestick Park in San Francisco, as each
team hit four home runs. The Braves four-baggers were
smacked by first baseman Joe Adcock in the second inning,
shortstop Roy McMillan and third baseman Eddie Mathews in
the fifth inning, and second baseman Frank Bolling in the
seventh frame. McMillan's came with no one on base while
the other three were two-run shots.

5. **CALIFORNIA ANGELS**

The Angels have played games using many names in their
history, playing in both Los Angeles and Anaheim. On June

16, 1966, they were known as the California Angels and beat the Minnesota Twins at Metropolitan Stadium in Bloomington, Minnesota, 7-2. All seven runs came on the four homers by shortstop Jim Fregosi in the fourth inning, first baseman Norm Siebern in the seventh, third baseman Frank Malzone in the ninth, and second baseman Bobby Knoop in the ninth.

6. LOS ANGELES DODGERS
Twenty years after the Angels, on September 19, 1986, the Los Angeles Dodgers beat the Cincinnati Reds at Riverfront Stadium in Cincinnati, 9-7, with four home runs by the infield. First baseman Greg Brock hit a solo shot in the second inning to start the scoring in the contest. Shortstop Dave Anderson connected in the seventh frame, third baseman Bill Madlock hit his in the eighth, and second baseman Steve Sax hit the last of the quartet in the ninth inning.

7. TORONTO BLUE JAYS
In 1989, the Toronto Blue Jays won the American League East Division title. On July 24, they beat the Texas Rangers in Arlington, 6-3, with all their runs scoring on home runs. Shortstop Tony Fernandez, the second batter of the game, plated the first runs of the contest with a two-run homer and third baseman Kelly Gruber followed with another home run back-to-back. First baseman Fred McGriff led off the third frame with a solo homer and, three batters later, shortstop Manuel Lee hit a two-run blast to complete the Jays scoring.

8. NEW YORK METS
For the second time, this feat occurred at Chicago's Wrigley Field. This time the visiting New York Mets pulled it off as they beat the Cubs, 10-6, on June 10, 1997. First baseman John Olerud homered in the third frame, shortstop Manny Alexander hit one in the fourth, third baseman Edgardo

Alfonzo slugged one in the eighth and third baseman Carlos Baerga finished with his in the ninth inning.

9. SAN DIEGO PADRES

On August 10, 2000, the Padres clobbered the Phillies at Philadelphia's Veterans' Stadium, 15-3. The clubbing infield that day was second baseman Bret Boone (third inning), shortstop Desi Relaford and third baseman Phil Nevin (both in the sixth) and first baseman Joe Vitiello (eighth inning). Phillies manager Terry Francona had had enough by the seventh when he was ejected for arguing a call down the right field line.

10. PHILADELPHIA PHILLIES

On September 23, 2004, the Phillies slid by the Florida Marlins, 9-8, with a run in the top of the tenth inning at Pro Player Stadium (now Dolphins Stadium) on a home run by shortstop Jimmy Rollins. This capped the infield quartet's homer bash, as previously in the contest first baseman Jim Thome hit one in the fifth inning and second baseman Chase Utley and third baseman David Bell hit homers in the seventh frame.

Take That! No, Take That!

Pitchers rarely hit home runs, although to listen to some of them, you would think they were Babe Ruth reincarnated. On August 20, 1901, the Chicago White Sox played the Senators at American League Field in Washington. In the top of the sixth inning, Sox hurler Clark Griffith, who would later own the Senators, hit the ball onto the porch of the clubhouse for a two-run home run off Case Patten. In the bottom of the next frame, Patten, not to be outdone by his mound opponent, hit the ball over the left field fence. This was the first time in the 20th century that pitchers homered off each other in the same game. Here are the other ten instances since then.

1. JOHNNY COUCH AND DOLF LUQUE

At the Baker Bowl in Philadelphia on August 18, 1925, the visiting Cincinnati Reds won both games of a doubleheader from the Phillies. In the first contest, Johnny Couch of the Phils smacked a four-bagger off Dolf Luque in the third inning. In the top of the sixth frame, Couch surrendered back-to-back homers to Luque and Elmer Smith. They accounted for the last two runs in the 7-5 Cincinnati victory.

2. **TED BLANKENSHIP AND MILT GASTON**

The St. Louis Browns (now the Baltimore Orioles) beat the Chicago White Sox, 5-4, at Sportsman's Park in St. Louis on April 18, 1927. Losing pitcher Ted Blankenship drove in all four runs for his team with a bases-loaded double in the fifth and a solo homer in the seventh. Milt Gaston, the winning hurler that day, hit a two-run home run in the bottom of the seventh, which more than counteracted Blankenship's tally in the top of the frame.

3. **RALPH BRANCA AND CLIFF CHAMBERS**

On June 8, 1950, the Pittsburgh Pirates barely held on to beat the visiting Brooklyn Dodgers at Forbes Field, 4-3. In the top of the third inning, Dodger hurler Ralph Branca hit a solo home run off Cliff Chambers to tie the score, 1-1. This, the first of Branca's two career homers, landed in the left field bullpen. In the bottom of the seventh inning, catcher Clyde McCullough and Chambers hit back-to-back solo homers. Chambers, a left-handed swinger, hit the ball into the left field bullpen. In the top of the ninth, Brooklyn scored two runs for the victory.

4. **DON LARSEN AND DICK BRODOWSKI**

The New York Yankees beat the Red Sox at Fenway Park in Boston, 13-6, on August 16, 1955. The two teams combined for seven home runs in the contest, with Yankee pitcher Don Larsen hitting a three-run shot to cap off a seven-run third frame. Dick Brodowski, who had come into the game to face Larsen, broke the latter's shutout bid in the bottom of the fifth inning with a two-run four-bagger. In addition to these blasts by the hurlers, there were also homers by Mickey Mantle and Ted Williams in the game.

5. ELI GRBA AND PEDRO RAMOS

Eli Grba and Pedro Ramos traded solo home runs in the fifth inning of a game played on May 12, 1961, at Metropolitan Stadium in Bloomington, Minnesota. The visiting Los Angeles Angels, in their first year of play, lost to the Minnesota Twins, in their first year after moving from Washington. Grba, charged with the loss in the contest, did not last through the sixth inning, while Ramos pitched into the ninth inning to earn the win, 5-4.

6. EARL WILSON AND BUSTER NARUM

On April 14, 1965, the Boston Red Sox played the second game of the season at D.C. Stadium (now known as RFK Stadium) against the Washington Senators. The scoring started with a two-run home run by Sox hurler Earl Wilson in the top of the third inning off Buster Narum. With two out in the bottom of the fifth and Boston ahead, 3-2, Narum hit a solo homer to tie the score. Those were the only four-baggers in the game, which was won by the Senators, 6-4, as the two squads split the two-game series.

7. TONY CLONINGER AND RAY SADECKI

On July 3, 1966, Atlanta Braves pitcher Tony Cloninger performed a feat that had never been done before when he hit two grand slams in the same game. He was the first National Leaguer and remains the only pitcher to perform this feat. The second granny came off San Francisco Giants relief pitcher Ray Sadecki, who entered the game in the third inning with the Braves ahead, 8-0. Cloninger, who pitched a complete game victory, surrendered a solo home run to Sadecki in the bottom of the fifth inning at Candlestick Park, San Francisco.

8. KEVIN GROSS AND FERNANDO VALENZUELA

The Los Angeles Dodgers hosted the Montreal Expos on May 14, 1990, and won, 3-2. Expos hurler Kevin Gross started the scoring in the game with a solo homer off Fernando Valenzuela in the top of the third inning. In the bottom of that frame, Valenzuela returned the favor by leading off the inning with his own solo home run. The Dodgers scored two more runs in the inning and Valenzuela only surrendered one more run before leaving after the eighth inning, earning the victory.

9. KEVIN FOSTER AND MARVIN FREEMAN

Denver's Coors Field was, for many years, a park that surrendered numerous runs and home runs. On May 23, 1995, Kevin Foster of the Chicago Cubs and Marvin Freeman of the Colorado Rockies exchanged homers in a 7-6 Cubs victory. Foster's solo shot in the third inning put the Cubs on the board for the first time in the game, but he surrendered his 3-1 lead in the bottom of the fourth inning when Freeman hit a three-run home run. The Cubs got those runs back in the next half inning and did not give up the lead after that.

10. KEVIN MILLWOOD AND DENNY STARK

On May 18, 2002, Denny Stark and the Colorado Rockies beat the Atlanta Braves and Kevin Millwood, 7-3. The first run of the game came on Millwood's solo homer in the top of the third inning at Coors Field. Stark hit his return shot as part of a four-run fourth inning off Millwood. In the eleven listed instances of this feat, the last two have been done at Coors Field in Denver. No other park has seen more than one.

They Say It's Your Birthday

On August 7, 2007, Barry Bonds of the San Francisco Giants hit career home run number 756 to pass Hank Aaron and become the all-time career leader. He had hit his first on June 4, 1986, while playing for the Pittsburgh Pirates. On the day that Bonds was born, July 24, 1964, there were only four sluggers with at least 500 home runs. That day, Hank Aaron had hit 355 and was seventeenth on the career list. Here are the top ten hitters on the all-time home run list on the day that Barry Bonds was born.

1. BABE RUTH

The Bambino held the career record of 714 from July 18, 1921, through April 8, 1974, when Hank Aaron hit his 715th career four-bagger. Ruth hit 33.6 homers for every 500 plate appearances in his career, which is second-best all-time, behind Mark McGwire, among sluggers with at least 300 home runs. Barry Bonds passed Ruth on the all-time career list on May 28, 2006, with a two-run homer in San Francisco, and thus moved into the number two spot on the list.

2. JIMMIE FOXX
The Beast hit 534 circuit clouts in his career and was second on the all-time list from August 16, 1940, to August 17, 1966, when Willie Mays passed him. Foxx hit 27.6 home runs for every 500 plate appearances in his career, which, when Foxx retired, was second best behind only Babe Ruth. Bonds passed Foxx, then tenth on the all-time list, on July 18, 2001, with the first of two homers that day in San Francisco.

3. TED WILLIAMS
Teddy Ballgame hit 521 home runs in his career with the Boston Red Sox. He held third place on the all-time list from August 10, 1960, when he passed Mel Ott, through June 27, 1966, when Willie Mays passed him. Williams hit 26.6 home runs for every 500 plate appearances in his career. Bonds passed Williams on May 30, 2001, with his second home run of the day in San Francisco, thus moving into eleventh place on the career list at the time.

4. MEL OTT
Master Melvin hit 511 homers in his long career with the New York Giants and was third on the all-time list when he retired in 1947, having moved into third place on May 9, 1945, when he passed Lou Gehrig. Ott, the National League career leader in four-baggers on this day in 1964, was less prolific than many of the other sluggers here, as he hit 22.5 homers for every 500 plate appearances in his career. Bonds passed Ott on May 19, 2001, with the first of three homers that day in Atlanta, and moved into a tie for fourteenth place all-time.

5. LOU GEHRIG
The Iron Horse, who played his entire career in his hometown of New York, hit 493 homers as a member of the Yankees.

When he retired in 1939, Gehrig was second on the all-time list, although Jimmie Foxx was closing in fast. Gehrig hit 25.5 homers for every 500 plate appearances in his career. Bonds passed Gehrig on September 28, 2000, in Los Angeles to move into seventeenth place on the career list.

6. STAN MUSIAL

Stan the Man hit 475 home runs in his career, all of which was spent with the St. Louis Cardinals. Musial was second in homers in National League history on Barry Bonds' birthday, behind only Mel Ott. Musial hit 18.7 home runs for every 500 plate appearances in his career and retired after the 1963 season. Bonds passed Musial on July 19, 2000, in San Francisco to move into eighteenth place all-time.

7. MICKEY MANTLE

The Commerce Comet was the active leader in home runs on July 24, 1964, with 438. Mantle would eventually hit 536 four-baggers by the end of the 1968 season, hitting 27 homers for every 500 plate appearances in his career. He is the top switch hitter on the career home run list. Bonds passed Mantle with the first of two homers in Arizona on July 26, 2001, and moved into ninth place on the career list.

8. (TIE) WILLIE MAYS

The Say Hey Kid had hit 435 of his 660 career homers by July 24, 1964. Mays is the godfather to Barry Bonds, and has been a mentor throughout Barry's life. Mays hit 26.4 home runs for every 500 plate appearances in his career, which lasted until 1973. Bonds passed Mays in San Francisco on April 13, 2004, to move into third place all-time with Willie in attendance at the game.

9. (TIE) EDDIE MATHEWS

Eddie Mathews had hit 435 homers and was tied with Willie Mays on the all-time list when Barry Bonds was born. Mathews, who would end with 512 blasts when he retired in 1968, hit 25.3 home runs for every 500 plate appearances in his career. Bonds passed Mathews in Atlanta on May 19, 2001, with his second homer of the game to move into thirteenth place all-time.

10. DUKE SNIDER

The Duke of Flatbush was tenth on the all-time list on July 24, 1964. He had hit the last of his 407 career homers 20 days before Bonds was born and hit 24.7 home runs for every 500 plate appearances in his career. Barry Bonds passed Snider in Arizona on September 14, 1998, to move into twenty-sixth place on the career list.

If I Had a Hammer

Hank Aaron hit 755 home runs in his 23-year major league career. He was the career home run record holder from April 8, 1974, when he passed Babe Ruth, until August 7, 2007, when Barry Bonds passed him. Here are some facts you might not know about Hammerin' Hank.

1. SINGLE GAME HOMERS
Aaron hit three home runs in one game only once in his career. On June 21, 1959, Aaron hit three two-run blasts in San Francisco in the first, sixth and seventh innings, as the Braves beat the Giants, 13-3. He hit a pair of homers in a game 61 times.

2. SINGLE SEASON HOMERS
Aaron never hit 50 home runs in any one season. He hit 47 in 1971 and at least 40 in eight different seasons. He slugged 44 homers four times and that total just happened to be his uniform number.

3. LOST A HOMER FOR A TEAMMATE
On May 26, 1959, Harvey Haddix of the Pittsburgh Pirates threw a perfect game for twelve innings in Milwaukee. With

no score in the bottom of the thirteenth frame, after Felix Mantilla reached on an error (thus ending the perfect game) and was sacrificed to second, Hank Aaron was intentionally walked. Joe Adcock then hit a home run into the left field seats. However, Aaron didn't know the ball left the park, so he returned to the dugout thinking that Mantilla's run ended the game. Adcock was called out for passing Aaron, which nullified the homer, but Mantilla scored on the play, Adcock was credited with a double, and the game ended in a 1-0, one hitter loss for Haddix.

4. BRAVES FRANCHISE LEADER

Okay, so this one seems easy—right? The trick is that Aaron hit 733 home runs for the Braves split between two cities, Milwaukee and Atlanta. He is not the career leader in either city because Eddie Mathews hit 452 in Milwaukee to Aaron's 398 and three players (Chipper Jones, Dale Murphy and Andruw Jones) have hit more than Aaron's 335 for the Atlanta edition of the club.

5. CAN I SEND A CAR FOR YOU?

Aaron hit 17 home runs off Hall of Fame pitcher Don Drysdale of the Dodgers. The first came on June 29, 1958, in Milwaukee, where Hank hit 11 off Drysdale. Aaron also hit five in Los Angeles and one in Atlanta. The 17 is the third-highest total by one batter off one pitcher in history. On days that Drysdale was scheduled to pitch against the Braves, Aaron probably wanted to send a limo for the hurler to ensure he got to the park!

6. NOT BAD FOR AN OLD GUY

Aaron hit 42 of his 755 home runs after he turned 40 years old, which places him in the top ten of sluggers in their forties. Barry Bonds and Carlton Fisk lead that list, each having hit more than 70 at that age. In 1973, at the age of 39, Aaron hit 40 home runs—once for each 9.8 at bats for the season. This was Aaron's most productive year for home runs and it came at an age when most players have already retired.

7. **MR. CONSISTENT**

The Hammer hit at least 20 home runs for 20 consecutive seasons. This is the record for most consecutive years by any batter. However, 20 homers for 20 years is only 400, barely half way to Aaron's career total. In 15 of those 20 seasons, Aaron actually hit at least 30 blasts, with one more year at 29.

8. **BRAVES SEASON LEADER MANY TIMES**

Aaron led the Braves team in home runs for 11 consecutive years from 1962 through 1972, although he tied for the lead in 1965 with Eddie Mathews. No other Brave has led the team for more consecutive seasons than Hank.

9. **LEAGUE LEADER**

Aaron led the National League for four seasons. He hit 44 in 1957, 44 again in 1963 (to tie with Willie McCovey of the Giants), 44 yet again in 1966, and 39 in 1967. In 1971, when he hit his career-high 47 dingers, Aaron placed second to Willie Stargell of the Pirates, who hit 48 long balls.

10. **HOME TOWN HERO**

Aaron is the single-season leader for the Braves in four-baggers hit at home. In 1971, when he hit 47 clouts, Aaron hit 31 of them at Atlanta Stadium. The second-highest total for a Brave at home is the 27 that Jeff Burroughs hit in 1977.

My Hand Is Tired

A good day for an umpire is one in which he is not noticed while on the field. One time that they might be noticed is when a ball flies over the fence and the umpire signals with a circular motion of his hand in the air, indicating that the batter may run the circuit of the bases on the home run. Here are the arbiters who have been behind the plate for the most home runs in history.

1. BRUCE FROEMMING
Bruce Froemming became the second umpire to work 5,000 major league games on August 16, 2006, matching the feat of Bill Klem. Froemming worked 5,162 games in the majors from 1971 through 2007, including three All Star Games and five World Series. He watched 2,194 regular season home runs from behind the catcher in that time.

2. JOE BRINKMAN
Joe Brinkman umpired in the big leagues from 1972 through 2006, and ran an umpire training school for many years in Florida. Brinkman umpired 4,505 regular season games (fifth place all-time), three World Series and three All Star Games and was the plate umpire for 2,121 home runs.

Umpire Bruce Froemming makes a call at home plate.
Major League Baseball

3. MIKE REILLY

Mike Reilly topped the 4,000 games worked plateau during
the 2007 season, just the 17th arbiter to reach that milestone.
Reilly started in the major leagues in 1977 and has worked
three All Star Games and four World Series. He has watched
2,076 regular season home runs from behind the plate.

4. DERRYL COUSINS

Derryl Cousins first came to the big leagues in 1979 and has
worked nearly 4,000 games since. He has also umpired three
All Star Games and three World Series. Cousins has been the
plate umpire for 2,042 home runs.

5. BILL KLEM

Hall of Famer Bill Klem worked more games than any other major league umpire in history with 5,369. He was a National League arbiter from 1905 through 1941 and umpired 18 World Series and two All Star Games. Klem umpired in the first Midsummer Classic in 1933, after he had been in the majors for 28 years. During his time in the big leagues, Klem was behind the plate for 2,022 home runs.

6. LARRY BARNETT

Larry Barnett, from Nitro, West Virgina, umpired in the major leagues from 1969 through 1999, totaling 4,290 games. He worked in four All Star Games and four World Series in his career. In his time behind the plate, batters hit 1,885 home runs.

7. TIM MCCLELLAND

Tim McClelland, who stands 6'6" tall, umpired his first major league game in 1981. He has worked in three All Star Games, four World Series, and 3,582 regular season games through 2008. McClelland has watched 1,849 home runs from behind the mask. He was behind the plate for George Brett's Pine Tar homer on July 24, 1983, which is chronicled elsewhere in this volume.

8. LARRY MCCOY

Larry McCoy umpired 4,023 major league games from 1970 through 1999. He also worked in three All Star Games and two World Series. He watched 1,847 home runs from behind the plate in his 30 years in the majors.

9. **ED MONTAGUE**

Ed Montague, son of a former major league player by the same name, worked his first big league game as an umpire in 1974. In 2007, he reached the top ten all-time in games worked and also has worked four All Star Games and six World Series. Montague has been behind the plate for 1,838 home runs since his debut.

10. **JERRY CRAWFORD**

Jerry Crawford, son of major league umpire Shag Crawford, started in the major leagues in 1976 and passed the 4,000-game milestone in 2007. He has also worked two All Star Games and five World Series. Crawford has been behind the plate for 1,834 home runs. Jerry's brother, Joe, is a long-time NBA referee. Shag Crawford saw 1,263 homers from behind the plate.

I Did *What?*

Many batters have hit a four-bagger and then have done something to lose the homer before completing the circuit of the bases. Here is a chronological list of those batter gaffes.

1. FRED COREY, RUBY LEGS
On September 23, 1880, pitcher Fred Corey of the National League's Worcester Ruby Legs hit an inside-the-park homer against the Boston Red Caps (now Atlanta Braves) but failed to touch third base. He was called out on appeal and was credited with a double. The Ruby Legs won anyway, 9-4.

2. BILL KEISTER, PHILLIES
In the top of the first inning on May 30, 1903, the Phillies had a runner on first base and two out. Bill Keister hit a ball off pitcher Henry Schmidt that got past the Brooklyn fielders into left-center field and Keister ran all the way around the bases for an inside-the-park home run. However, umpire Jim Johnstone ruled that he cut second base (not touching it) and Keister ended up with an RBI single. This call hurt the Phillies as Brooklyn won the game, 4-3.

3. JACK DUNN, GIANTS

On October 4, 1903, in the second game of a doubleheader on the last day of the season, Jack Dunn of the Giants homered. However, umpire Jim Johnstone called him out for missing first base. This and other protests caused the arbiter to forfeit the game to St. Louis. Dunn later owned the Baltimore Orioles minor league team and signed a young man named George Ruth to play for the squad. Ruth acquired the nickname "Babe" and went on to a Hall of Fame career.

4. BUTCH HENLINE, PHILLIES

It was the bottom of the tenth in the first game of a Memorial Day doubleheader in Philadelphia on May 30, 1922. Butch Henline batted with the score tied and runners on first and third. He hit the ball into the left field bleachers for a game-ending homer. However, after Tilly Walker scored from third, Henline stopped at second. Thus he gave up a homer for a double. He might have thought the old rule was still in effect where he did not get credit for a home run on this play—that rule was rescinded for the 1920 season and if Henline had completed running the circuit he would have another home run on his record.

5. DEL BISSONETTE, ROBINS (NOW DODGERS)

In the first game of a Memorial Day doubleheader on May 30, 1930, Dodger Del Bissonette batted against Claude Willoughby of the Phillies in the bottom of the fourth inning with runners on first and second. As Bissonette's fly ball neared the Ebbets Field fence, Babe Herman, fearing a catch, stopped between first and second base. Bissonette didn't see Herman and passed him. He was called out by umpire Cy Pfirman and was credited with a two-RBI single.

6. GLENN WRIGHT, ROBINS (NOW DODGERS)

On September 15, 1930, in the bottom of the second with runners on first and second, Glenn Wright hit the ball to right-center. It looked like it might be caught so Babe Herman slowed up as he neared second. The ball bounced over the fence for a home run, but Wright had his head down as he ran between first and second. Because of this, he passed Herman and was called out. Wright lost a homer but still knocked in two runs as the Robins beat the Reds, 13-5. Yes, you read this correctly—Babe Herman was passed twice during the 1930 season on apparent homers!

7. LOU GEHRIG, YANKEES

In the first inning at Griffith Stadium, Washington, D.C., on April 26, 1931, with Lyn Lary on first and two out, Lou Gehrig hit a home run into the centerfield bleachers. However, the ball caromed back to the centerfielder. Lary returned to the dugout, evidently thinking the ball was caught. Gehrig was declared out for passing the runner and lost the homer. He ended the year tied for the lead in homers with Babe Ruth.

8. ETHAN ALLEN, CARDINALS

On June 29, 1933, in the top of the second inning, Redbird outfielder Ethan Allen hit an inside-the-park homer to deep left-center field at the Polo Grounds. However, he batted out of turn, so he lost the homer and the proper batter, Joe Medwick, was called out. The drive came off Watty Clark with no one on and one out. The Redbirds won the contest in spite of this gaffe, 7-3.

9. TONY OLIVA, TWINS

Tony Oliva of Minnesota lost a home run due to a base running blunder on April 21, 1967. Playing in Detroit in the third inning, Cesar Tovar was the runner at first base. Oliva hit the ball out of the park off Denny McLain, but then passed Tovar between first and second. He was credited with a single and one RBI for scoring Tovar. The Tigers won, 12-4.

10. DON BUFORD, ORIOLES

On July 18, 1969, Don Buford hit the ball into the right field seats at Fenway Park in the eighth inning. Tony Conigliaro leaped and fell into the stands, but did not have the ball when he came up. The first base umpire, Bob Stewart, gave no signal. Dave May, running at first, hesitated, then started back to first base. Buford passed him and May was called out while Buford circled the bases. A five-minute argument followed. Earl Weaver argued about Stewart's delayed home run call. Eventually, Buford was credited with a run-scoring single, and May with a run scored, even though those events never actually happened on the field. Home plate umpire Red Flaherty allegedly called May out, which was why he stopped running and never crossed the plate. The hit came off Ray Jarvis, who was ahead 6-0 at the time, and May's run was the only tally of the game for the Orioles.

No Way, I Did Not Do That!

We have so many batter blunders that we expanded it to two lists!

1. DALTON JONES, TIGERS

On July 9, 1970, Dalton Jones pinch-hit for Jim Price with the bases loaded in the seventh inning at Tiger Stadium. Jones hammered the 2-2 pitch into the upper deck in right field for a grand slam. However, Jones passed Don Wert between first and second and was called out, thus being credited with a three-RBI single. Boston's Vicente Romo had entered the game to face Jones and gave up the blast which, officially, never happened. The Tigers won the game despite the bungle by Jones, 7-3.

2. CARLOS MAY, WHITE SOX

Carlos May of the Chicago White Sox homered in the top of the first inning of the second game of a doubleheader on April 7, 1971. The blow came with two runners on base, and one out, off Rollie Fingers in Oakland. May did not touch home plate and was out on appeal; he was credited with a triple and two RBIs. The Sox won the contest, 12-4.

3. ED GOODSON, GIANTS
On June 19, 1974, Ed Goodson hit a home run in the third inning off Bob Gibson at St. Louis with Garry Maddox on first and no one out. Unfortunately, he passed Maddox between first and second base. Goodson was credited with a single and a run batted in as the Giants won, 5-4.

4. TIM McCARVER, PHILLIES
On the day celebrated as the Bicentennial of the United States, July 4, 1976, catcher Tim McCarver of the Phillies hit a grand slam in the second inning of the first game of a doubleheader at Pittsburgh. The 375-foot homer came off Larry Demery and the runner at first, Garry Maddox, retreated toward first thinking the ball might be caught at the wall. After rounding first base, McCarver passed Maddox and was called out. He received credit for a single and three runs batted in.

5. RALPH GARR, WHITE SOX
Ralph Garr of the White Sox homered off Minnesota's Paul Thormodsgard in Minneapolis on June 24, 1977. It came in the third inning with two men on and no one out. Jim Essian, the runner on first, thought the ball might be caught by the Twins' right fielder, Dan Ford, so he retreated toward first base. Garr was watching the flight of the ball and passed Essian after rounding the bag. He was credited with a single and two runs batted in.

6. LEE LACY, PIRATES
On May 14, 1982, Pittsburgh's Lee Lacy batted in the bottom of the eighth inning as the first batter to face Tom Hume of the Reds. The bases were loaded with no outs and Lacy hit one of Hume's pitches out of the park. However, in the celebration during his run around the bases, Lacy passed Omar

Moreno between first and second. He is credited with a single and three runs batted in. Luckily, Moreno's run won the game for the Pirates 8-7.

7. BOBBY MEACHAM, YANKEES

On April 11, 1985, Bobby Meacham batted in the top of the fourth inning in Texas with two runners on and one out. He homered off Frank Tanana but neither Meacham nor the runner at first, Willie Randolph, expected the ball to leave the yard. While Meacham was running toward and around first base, Randolph was headed back to the bag to tag up. They collided just past first base and Meacham was credited with a two-run single.

8. MICHAEL TUCKER, ROYALS

Michael Tucker hit a long fly to center in Oakland with Mike Caruso the runner at second base in the top of the tenth inning on July 6, 2002. Terrence Long caught the ball at the wall but he snow-coned the ball and lost it over the fence for a homer when he hit the wall. Caruso started to tag up as Tucker approached second. Tucker stopped but Caruso passed him going back to the bag. Tucker was called out for passing the runner and he lost a homer but was credited with an RBI-single that gave the Royals a 4-3 victory over the Athletics.

9. JAVY LOPEZ, ORIOLES

On April 16, 2006, Javy Lopez of the Orioles hit a home run to left-center in the second inning of a game at Camden Yards as Darin Erstad attempted to catch the ball at the wall. The runner on first, Miguel Tejada, thinking the ball was caught, returned toward the bag and Lopez rounded first and passed Tejada. Lopez was called out and Tejada scored on the play, giving Lopez an RBI single over the wall. The Angels beat the Orioles, 9-3.

10. **ROBIN VENTURA, METS**

This is a case of teammates causing the batter to lose a homer—in fact, a grand slam. On October 17, 1999, in game five of the National League Championship Series, the Braves had taken a 3-2 lead in the top of the 15th inning. However, after an intentional walk to load the bases, Todd Pratt walked to push across the tying run for the Mets. Robin Ventura came to the plate with a chance to win the game and he hit the ball over the right centerfield fence for an apparent game-ending grand slam. However, once each runner advanced a base, thus scoring the winning run, Pratt stopped and ran towards Ventura to give him a big hug. Ventura had rounded first base on his home run trot and motioned for the other runners to continue around the bases. Since each runner only advanced one base, Ventura was credited with an RBI-single. It would have been the first game-ending grand slam in the history of post-season.

Hail to the Chief!

S ince the start of the National League in 1876, 26 people have held the office of president of the United States. The lengths of these administrations run from less than one season for James A. Garfield to the 12 seasons for Franklin D. Roosevelt. Many chief executives were baseball fans, taking time to go to games while in office. Here is a list of presidential administrations with at least 10,000 homers hit during their time in office.

1. GEORGE W. BUSH (41,412)

George (the son), the former owner of the Texas Rangers, took office in 2001 and has been president during the height of the most prolific era in home run history. Alex Rodriguez has hit the most dingers during the Bush administration with 364. This total is the most by any single slugger during one presidential administration.

2. WILLIAM J. CLINTON (37,304)

Bill Clinton served as president for the 1993 through 2000 baseball seasons. His eight seasons include the beginning of the home run surge that started in 1994. Ken Griffey, Jr. hit

351 four-baggers during the Clinton administration while Sammy Sosa hit 349.

3. **RONALD W. REAGAN (26,772)**

The Reagan presidency ran from the 1981 season through the 1988 season. Reagan, the actor turned politician, also served as governor of California and once played pitcher Grover Cleveland Alexander in a movie. Mike Schmidt (259 home runs) and Dale Murphy (255) are the individual leaders during the Reagan administration.

4. **DWIGHT D. EISENHOWER (17,351)**

Dwight Eisenhower is rumored to have played professional baseball as a young man under an assumed name. He is more famous as the Supreme Allied Commander during D-Day in 1944. Eisenhower served as president from the 1953 season through the 1960 campaign and Eddie Mathews smacked 313 homers during Ike's administration.

5. **RICHARD M. NIXON (16,961)**

Richard Nixon served as president from the 1969 season through August 8, 1974, when he resigned the office. Hank Aaron led the major leagues with 218 home runs while Willie Stargell hit 203 during the Nixon administration.

6. **FRANKLIN D. ROOSEVELT (15,362)**

FDR was elected president four times, more than any other person. He served in office from the 1933 season through his death on April 12, 1945, just five days before the start of the season. Jimmie Foxx hit 353 four-baggers and Mel Ott smacked 336 while Roosevelt was chief executive. Foxx's total is the second highest for any single batter during one presidential administration.

7. JAMES E. CARTER (13,120)

Jimmy Carter served one term as president, from the 1977 through 1980 seasons and his administration saw more home runs than any other single-term administration in history. Since leaving office, Carter, the former Georgia governor, has attended many Braves games in Atlanta. Mike Schmidt (152), Jim Rice (148), and George Foster (147) led the majors during the Carter administration.

8. GEORGE H.W. BUSH (12,821)

Another one-term president, George (the father) served as president for the 1989 through 1992 seasons. Fred McGriff hammered 137 four-baggers and Mark McGwire 136 during these four years.

9. HARRY S TRUMAN (12,683)

Harry Truman became president upon the death of Franklin Roosevelt on April 12, 1945, just five days before the season started, and served through the 1952 season. Ralph Kiner clobbered 294 circuit drives during the Truman years.

10. LYNDON B. JOHNSON (12,487)

Like Truman, Lyndon Johnson assumed the office of president on the death of his predecessor, John Kennedy. Johnson's administration encompassed the 1964 through 1968 seasons. Willie Mays whacked 181 home runs during this time while Harmon Killebrew slugged 174.

Love, American (League) Style

For most broadcasters, the home run call is their signature moment. Indeed, many times it is the one phrase that is remembered long after that person is no longer on the air. Here are the calls from some American League broadcasters.

1. "IT IS GOING, IT IS GOING, IT IS GONE. HOW ABOUT THAT!"

Mel Allen, the longtime voice of the New York Yankees, was a pioneer of broadcasting baseball on the radio. He worked for the Yankees from 1939 through 1964 and was known as the "Voice of the Yankees." For many years Allen was the voice of baseball's weekly highlight show, *This Week in Baseball*. He received the Ford C. Frick Award for major contributions to baseball as a broadcaster in 1978.

2. "LONG GONE!"

Ernie Harwell broadcast games for the Brooklyn Dodgers, New York Giants, and Baltimore Orioles. However, he is best known as the long-time voice of the Detroit Tigers and winner of the 1981 Ford C. Frick Award. In addition to broadcasting, Harwell wrote essays, including his best-known work, *Baseball—A Game for All America.*

3. "AIN'T THE BEER COLD!"

Chuck Thompson broadcast major league games in seven decades. He worked home games for both the Phillies and Athletics in Philadelphia in 1947–48. Then he moved to Baltimore in 1949 to work for the minor league Orioles. When the St. Louis Browns moved to Baltimore, Thompson stayed and worked into the 21st century with the Birds.

4. "GET UP, GET UP, GET OUTTA HERE! IT'S GONE!"

Bob Uecker joined the Milwaukee Brewers radio crew in 1971 and continues to work with the club into the 21st century. The former catcher made a name for himself as a comedian, appearing on "The Tonight Show with Johnny Carson" many times and starring in his own network television show. Uecker's call is so popular in Milwaukee that it can be found on the home of Bernie the Brewer above left field at Miller Park. Although the Brewers are now a National League team, they spent more of their time in the American League.

5. "IT WILL FLY AWAY! MY, OH MY!"

Dave Niehaus has broadcast Mariners baseball since the club's inception in 1977. Before moving to Seattle, Niehaus worked for the Angels and Dodgers. He started his major league career on the Armed Forces Network, broadcasting Dodgers and Yankees games. Niehaus threw out the Ceremonial Pitch for the Inaugural Game at Safeco Field on July 15, 1999, and was presented with the Frick Award in 2008. He is also known for his call on a grand slam: "Get out the rye bread and mustard grandma, 'cause it's grand salami time!"

6. "TOUCH 'EM ALL!"

John Gordon broadcast games for the Baltimore Orioles (1970–73) and New York Yankees (1982–86) before moving to the Twins booth in 1987. He has also broadcast in the minor leagues and for the University of Virginia.

7. "YOU CAN PUT IT ON THE BOARD . . . YES!"

Ken "Hawk" Harrelson played in the majors for four teams from 1963 through 1971, hitting 131 home runs. He started his broadcasting career with the Red Sox in 1975, moved to the White Sox booth in 1982 for three seasons, and then decided to work in the front office of the Chicago team. He returned to broadcasting with the Yankees for the 1987–88 seasons and has been back in Chicago since 1991.

8. "THAT BALL IS HISTORY!"

Eric Nadel has been a part of the Texas Rangers broadcast crew since 1979 and the lead announcer since 1995. He has broadcast minor league hockey and women's professional basketball. Nadel also produced and recorded a series of features called "A Page from Baseball's Past" that run on the Rangers network.

9. "GOODBYE, BASEBALL!"

Rick Rizzs called games for the Detroit Tigers from 1992 through 1994 but is best known for his time with the Seattle Mariners. Rizzs worked in the Seattle booth both before and after his Detroit stint, 1983–91 and 1995 to the present.

10. "THAT BALL IS HIGH! IT IS FAR! IT IS GONE!"

John Sterling has worked on the Yankees radio broadcasts since 1989. He had broadcast Braves games in the 1980s and has hosted various radio shows in New York and Atlanta.

Love, National (League) Style

The Senior Circuit has a tradition of announcers with long tenures with one club and, like their brethren in the American League, some memorable home run calls. Here are some of the best calls from the National League.

1. "OPEN THE WINDOW, AUNT MINNIE, HERE IT COMES!"

Rosey Roswell broadcast Pirates games from 1936 through 1954. He partnered with Bob Prince for seven years and the pair thought of themselves as entertainers, often using colorful and humorous phrases in their broadcasts. At times, they would use a breaking glass sound to punctuate Roswell's call. He also wrote four books of humor and poetry.

2. "BYE BYE, BABY"

Russ Hodges broadcast games for the Reds, Cubs, Senators, and Yankees before joining the New York Giants staff in 1949. He worked for the Giants in New York and San Francisco for 22 years. Hodges won the Ford C. Frick Award for major contributions to baseball as a broadcaster posthumously in 1980.

3. "IT MIGHT BE . . . IT COULD BE . . . IT IS! A HOME RUN!"

Harry Carey broadcast more than 8,300 major league games in his career for the St. Louis Cardinals, Oakland Athletics, Chicago White Sox, and Chicago Cubs. Although sometimes controversial, he was always a fan favorite and his horned-rimmed glasses are now a trademark at Wrigley Field. Carey won the Ford C. Frick Award in 1989.

4. "HEY, HEY!"

Jack Brickhouse began broadcasting both Cubs and White Sox games in 1940 by recreating the action from the studio. He worked over 5,000 Cubs games through the 1981 season and received the Ford C. Frick Award in 1983. He also worked four World Series, five All Star Games, and for 24 years as the voice of the Chicago Bears of the NFL.

5. "YOU CAN KISS IT GOODBYE"

Bob Prince broadcast games for the Pittsburgh Pirates from 1948 through 1975. He also worked briefly for the Houston Astros. Nicknamed "The Gunner" for his rapid-fire style, Prince won the Ford C. Frick Award posthumously in 1986.

6. "SEE! YOU! LATER!"

Bob Carpenter has broadcast games for the Cardinals, Rangers, Mets, Twins, and ESPN. Since 2006, he has worked for the Washington Nationals as the play-by-play announcer on television. His signature call gained national prominence in 1998 when Mark McGwire broke the single-season home run record and Carpenter was broadcasting for the Redbirds.

7. "TELL IT GOODBYE!"

Lon Simmons, the 2004 Ford C. Frick awardee, broadcast games in the Bay Area for 41 years. He worked for the San Francisco Giants when they moved to California and later for the Oakland Athletics. Simmons also broadcast games of the NFL's San Francisco 49ers.

8. "WATCH THAT BABY . . . OUTTA HERE!"

Harry Kalas started his big league career with the Houston Astros in 1965 and moved to Philadelphia in 1971, where he continues to work. He paired with Hall of Fame outfielder Richie Ashburn for 26 years. Kalas won the Ford C. Frick Award in 2002.

9. "BONSOIR, ELLE EST PARTIE!"

Rodger Brulotte worked for the Montreal Expos in many capacities. He started in 1969 in the scouting department, worked in public relations, marketing and served as the team's traveling secretary for two years. For many years, Brulotte worked on the French radio and television broadcasts for the Expos. His phrase means "See ya, it's out of here!"

10. "SE VA . . . SE VA . . . YYYYYYYYYYYY DESPÍDELA CON UN BESO"

Jaime Jarrin, the "Spanish Voice of the Dodgers," has broadcast Los Angeles games since 1959. He has worked many years broadcasting the World Series and All Star Games on Spanish radio and was the coordinator of Spanish broadcasting for the 1984 Olympic Games in Los Angeles. His call translates as "It's going . . . it's going . . . you can kiss it goodbye."

Triple Crown Winners

A batter wins the Triple Crown if he leads his league in home runs, runs batted in, and batting average in the same season. Runs batted in became an official statistic in 1920, but baseball historians have researched runs batted in before that time and completed players' records in that statistic. The following players have been retroactively awarded the Triple Crown title based on that research: Tip O'Neill (American Association, 1887), Hugh Duffy (National League, 1894), Nap Lajoie (American League, 1901), and Ty Cobb (American League, 1909). Contemporaries did not recognize them since runs batted in were not counted at the time. Here are the recognized Triple Crown players since 1920.

1. ROGERS HORNSBY

In 1922, second baseman Rogers Hornsby was appointed player/manager of the St. Louis Cardinals in mid-season. At the end of the campaign, Hornsby led the National League in homers with 42 (Cy Williams of the Phillies was second with 26), in runs batted in with 152 (Irish Meusel of the New York Giants was second with 132), and in batting average with a .401 mark (Ray Grimes of the Cubs was second with .354). Thus Hornsby, the first Triple Crown winner, far outdistanced the runner-up in each of the three categories. The Rajah was the first National League player to hit at least 40 homers in a season. Three years later, Hornsby led the NL with 39 homers, 143 RBIs, and a batting average of .403 to win his second Triple Crown.

2. JIMMIE FOXX

Jimmie Foxx, known as "The Beast" for his physique, became the first American League Triple Crown winner in 1933 when he hit 48 circuit drives, drove in 163 runs, and hit .356 for the Philadelphia Athletics. Foxx led the AL in homers the previous year and would lead the majors for the decade of the 1930s. Foxx was the first player to hit at least 200 home runs for each of two teams when he slugged 302 for the Athletics and 222 for the Boston Red Sox. He became the second batter with 500 career homers on September 24, 1940, when he hit his milestone against his former team, the Athletics.

3. CHUCK KLEIN

Chuck Klein led the National League in homers four times: 1929 and 1931 through 1933. In 1933, he also led the circuit in batting average and RBIs to win the Triple Crown. That season remains the only time that both league leaders won the Triple Crown. Klein hit 28 homers, collected 120 runs batted in, and hit .368 for the season to top the league in the three statistical categories. He played most of his career for the Phillies, whose home park, the Baker Bowl, was well suited to left-handed pull hitters like Klein. Having led the NL in homers in four of five years, Klein found himself traded to the Cubs after the 1933 season. In 1936, he whacked four home runs in one game at Forbes Field in Pittsburgh to become the fourth batter to accomplish the feat. At the time, only Rogers

Hornsby and Babe Ruth had hit at least three homers in one game at the huge Pittsburgh ballpark.

4. LOU GEHRIG

The year after two players won their league's Triple Crown, Lou Gehrig of the Yankees repeated the performance in the American League. To earn that 1934 honor, Gehrig topped three different players for the three titles by considerable margins, as he hit 49 home runs (to Jimmie Foxx's 44), drove in 165 runs (to Hal Trosky's 142), and hit .363 (to Charlie Gehringer's .356). Gehrig was the first American League player to slug four homers in one game when he performed the feat in 1932. When he was forced to retire due to illness in 1939, his 493 career four-baggers placed him second on the all-time list behind former teammate Babe Ruth.

5. JOE MEDWICK

The last National League player to win the Triple Crown was Joe Medwick in 1937. The Cardinals outfielder hit 31 homers, drove in 154 runs, and hit .374 for the season. In addition, he led the league in runs scored (111), hits (237), doubles (56), and slugging average (.641). His 1937 totals represent his career highs in each of the Triple Crown statistics. He was voted the NL Most Valuable Player for 1937 and elected to the Hall of Fame in 1968.

6. TED WILLIAMS

Ted Williams of the Boston Red Sox won the American League Triple Crown twice—the only AL player to perform the feat multiple times. In 1942, Williams slugged 36 home runs, drove in 137, and hit .356 for the season while five years later he smacked 32 homers, had 114 runs batted in, and batted .343. None of those figures were career highs for Williams, as he had hit .406 in 1941 and achieved his career best with 43 home runs and 159 runs batted in during the 1949 season. In 1949, Williams lead the AL in homers, tied for the lead in RBIs with his teammate, Vern Stephens, and finished second behind George Kell (.3429 to .3428) for the batting title, thus missing an unprecedented third Triple Crown by just one hit! Williams won two AL Most Valuable Player Awards (1946 and 1949) but neither came in his Triple Crown seasons. Teddy Ballgame was elected to the Hall of Fame in 1966.

7. MICKEY MANTLE

Mickey Mantle had his career year in 1956 as he led the American League with 52 homers, 130 runs batted in, and a .353 batting average. This was the first of two seasons that Mantle would hit at least 50 homers, as he smacked 54 in 1961 to finish second to Roger Maris that season. Mantle won the first of three American League Most Valuable Player Awards in 1956, also taking home the trophy in 1957 and 1962. Mantle hit more home runs than any other switch hitter in history (536); indeed, only one other switcher has topped the 500 mark, Eddie Murray with 504. Mantle was elected to the Hall of Fame in 1974.

8. FRANK ROBINSON

Frank Robinson played the first ten years of his Hall of Fame career with the Cincinnati Reds, winning the National League Rookie of the Year Award in 1956 and the NL Most Valuable Player Award in 1961. Robinson was traded to the Baltimore Orioles after the 1965 season and he proved that to be a very bad move (for Cincinnati) by leading the American League in homers (49), runs batted in (122), and batting average (.316) and helping the Orioles to win their first World Series in 1966. He won the Triple Crown, the AL Most

Valuable Player Award, and the World Series Most Valuable Player Award in the same season.

9. CARL YASTRZEMSKI

For the second consecutive year, an American League player won the Triple Crown in 1967. This time it was Carl Yastrzemski of the Boston Red Sox with 44 homers (tied with Harmon Killebrew of the Twins), 121 runs batted in and a .326 batting average to become the most recent player to win the Triple Crown. The Red Sox and Twins fought to the last day of the season for the AL championship, with Yaz driving in six runs with seven hits in eight at bats in the two-game series between the contenders to end the season. Yastrzemski was named the league's 1967 Most Valuable Player and elected to the Hall of Fame in 1989.

10. NEAR MISS BY JIM RICE

Only nine players have won the Triple Crown. The most recent player to lead in two categories and place at least third in the other was Jim Rice of the Red Sox in 1978. Rice hammered 46 homers and drove in 139 runs to lead the American League in those categories. His .315 batting average was 18 points behind Rod Carew and put Rice in third place behind Al Oliver, who hit .324.

Another Year, Another Homer

One of the criteria for consideration for election to the Hall of Fame is consistency at a high level for a long time. The batters on this list hit at least one major league home run for 22 or more consecutive seasons. In 2007, Barry Bonds joined the list with his 22nd consecutive season with at least one home run. Unless noted, these seasons represent the player's entire career.

1. RICKEY HENDERSON, 25
Rickey Henderson is more famous as a base stealer than a slugger. However, he holds the record for the most consecutive seasons with at least one homer with 25, and most games leading off the first inning with a home run at 81 times. Henderson homered in each season from 1979 through 2003.

2. TY COBB, 24
"The Georgia Peach," like Henderson, is known more for his running ability than his slugging prowess. It is interesting that neither player at the top of this list is known primarily as a home run hitter. Cobb homered in 24 straight seasons from 1905 through 1928.

Rickey Henderson coiled and ready to run.
National Baseball Hall of Fame Library

3. HANK AARON, 23

Hank "The Hammer" Aaron, who hit 755 career four-baggers, hit at least one home run in 23 consecutive seasons from 1954 through 1976. In fact, he slugged at least ten in each year of that 23-year span. Aaron started his career with the Milwaukee Braves and moved with them to Atlanta. In 1975, Aaron returned to Milwaukee to play for the American League Brewers, thus ending his career in the same city as he started, but in the other league.

4. CARL YASTRZEMSKI, 23
Yaz played his entire 23-year career with the Boston Red Sox from 1961 through 1983. He is one of three players on this list who played for only one team, along with Al Kaline and Brooks Robinson.

5. RUSTY STAUB, 23
Daniel Joseph Staub, known as "Rusty" due to his red hair, played for five teams in his career and homered at least once in 23 straight years from 1963 through 1985. While he played in Montreal, the French-speaking fans referred to him as "Le Grande Orange."

6. CARLTON FISK, 23
Carlton Fisk played two games for the Red Sox in 1969 before returning to the majors in 1971 with Boston, and homered at least once in every season from 1971 through 1993. After playing for the Red Sox through the 1980 season, he signed with the Chicago White Sox, where he played through the end of his career.

7. AL KALINE, 22
Al Kaline played his entire career with the Detroit Tigers and hit 399 four-baggers in 22 years. In his first season, 1953, he played only 30 games and had seven hits but one of those was a home run to start his string of seasons, which lasted through the 1974 campaign.

8. **BROOKS ROBINSON, 22**

Brooks Robinson played all or parts of 23 seasons for the Baltimore Orioles. In 1955, he played in only six games at the end of September and did not homer, starting his skein in 1956 and hitting at least one home run every year through 1977.

9. **WILLIE MCCOVEY, 22**

Willie McCovey played for the San Francisco Giants, San Diego Padres, Oakland Athletics, and finished with the Giants. In his 11 games in the American League at the end of the 1976 season, McCovey did not homer but he had smacked seven for the Padres earlier in the season to continue his streak, which started in 1959 and lasted through 1980.

10. **TONY PEREZ, 22**

Tony Perez played 12 games in 1964 for the Cincinnati Reds before hitting his first home run in 1965. He also homered for the Montreal Expos, Boston Red Sox, and Philadelphia Phillies through the 1986 season.

I Never Saw
That Before

Every time you walk into a ballpark, you have a chance to see something happen on the field that you have never seen before. You never know when a batter might hit for the cycle, a pitcher may throw a no-hitter, or a ball might roll into a fielder's jersey (I saw that happen to Ryan Zimmerman at RFK Stadium). The events in this list are unique in the history of the game—they have only happened once since 1876.

1. ALL STAR GRAND SLAM
Many players have homered in the All Star Game since it started in 1933. Stan Musial is the career leader with six circuit drives in the Midsummer Classic. However, only one batter has hit a four-bagger with the bases loaded: Fred Lynn. Lynn had already hit three career All Star homers when he batted in the third inning of the 1983 game. The American League had scored three runs in the inning and had the bases loaded with two out when Lynn smacked his slam. The AL won the contest, 13-3.

2. LIKE FATHER, LIKE SON
The Ken Griffeys, Senior and Junior, are the only father and son pair to homer in the same game, having hit back-to-back

shots for the Seattle Mariners on September 14, 1990, off Kirk McCaskill. The clouts came in the first inning of a game played in Anaheim and won by the Angels, 7-5. Senior was on the Mariners roster during September 1990 and the 1991 season. The only other father/son duo who played on the same team is Tim Raines, Senior and Junior, for the Baltimore Orioles. On October 4, 2001, Senior started in left field and Junior in center for the Birds. They repeated the feat the next day but neither homered in their short time together.

3. RUTH OUT-HOMERS THE LEAGUE
In 1920, Babe Ruth broke his own single-season record of 29, set the previous year, by hitting 54 long balls and no other American League club hit more than 50. Thus, Ruth alone hit more home runs than each of the other seven teams in the league. In fact, he out-homered seven of the eight National League clubs—only the Phillies out-slugged the Bambino with 64 circuit drives.

4. I'M A PITCHER, I'M A SLUGGER
Pitcher Dave Eiland made his major league debut with the New York Yankees on August 3, 1988, in Milwaukee. The first batter he faced, Paul Molitor, hit a solo homer off Eiland. After the 1991 season, Eiland signed with the San Diego Padres and pitched his first game in the National League on April 10, 1992. He batted for the first time in the majors in the bottom of the second inning with two out and a runner on second base. Eiland proceeded to homer in his first at bat and became the first and only player to surrender a home run to his first batter faced, and hit one in his first at bat in the majors.

5. LET'S TAKE A LOOK AT THE VIDEO TAPE
On August 28, 2008, Major League Baseball instituted an instant replay system in games to decide on home runs calls.

There are only three situations in which the replay can be used: (1) Was the potential homer fair or foul? (2) Did a fan interfere with a potential homer? (3) Did a potential homer go over the fence? On September 26, Bengie Molina of the Giants hit a fly ball that hit the wall in right field at AT&T Park in the sixth inning with one runner on base. The umpires called it in play and not a homer. Emmanuel Burriss pinch-ran for Molina at first base and then Giants skipper Bruce Bochy asked the umpires about the call. The arbiters decided to use the replay system and decided that it was a home run. Burriss ran the bases to score the run. Therefore, Molina gets credit for a homer and two runs batted in but *no run scored!* When Burriss returned to the dugout after scoring what most people might consider as Molina's run, Bengie shook Burriss' hand and said: "Good swing!"

6. LEADING FROM BEHIND
In 1997, Mark McGwire split his season between the Athletics in the American League and the Cardinals in the Nationals League. Before he was traded at the end of July, Big Mac hit 34 home runs for the Athletics. After moving to the other league, McGwire hit 34 homers for the Redbirds. He led neither league in home runs that season, but, remarkably, his 58 total dingers led the majors. This is the only instance in history where a slugger led the majors but led neither league in homers for a season.

7. OUTHITTING THE OPPOSITION
There have been many pitchers who have thrown no-hitters in their careers. There have also been a lot of hurlers who have hit multiple home runs in one game. However, only Rick Wise has combined those two feats in the same game. On June 23, 1971, Wise pitched for the Philadelphia Phillies against the Reds at Riverfront Stadium in Cincinnati, winning the contest, 4-0. Wise hit two home runs and drove in three

runs in the game as he allowed the Big Red Machine no hits and only one walk. The opposition included the all-time hit leader, Pete Rose, two Hall of Famers, Johnny Bench and Tony Perez, and a National League Most Valuable Player, George Foster.

8. PINCH-HIT GRAND SLAM DEBUT
On August 31, 2005, Jeremy Hermida made his big league debut with the Florida Marlins in a game against the St. Louis Cardinals. In the bottom of the seventh inning, Hermida pinch-hit for pitcher Brian Moehler with the bases loaded and no one out. He proceeded to sock a pinch-hit grand slam in his first major league at bat—the only player to perform this feat in history.

9. HOW MANY TEAMS?
In 2002, Alfonso Soriano hit a home run in the All Star Game while representing the New York Yankees on the American League team. Two years later, as a member of the Texas Rangers, he homered for the second time in All Star competition. In 2007, he represented the Chicago Cubs on the National League All Star roster and homered for the third time in the Midsummer Classic. He is the only player to hit a four-bagger while representing three different teams in the All Star Game.

10. GREAT START! WHAT? AGAIN?
Bob Nieman played 12 seasons in the major leagues. He made his big league debut on September 14, 1951, playing left field for the St. Louis Browns (now the Baltimore Orioles) at Fenway Park in Boston. In the second inning, he batted for the first time and socked a solo homer, one of many players to homer in their debut plate appearance. However, Nieman batted again in the next inning and hit a two-run home run to accomplish a unique feat. No other player has ever hit home runs in his first two major league at bats.

It's Outta Here—
You're Outta Here!

Through the years, many players have homered in a game, and then later been ejected by an umpire for some infraction. On June 28, 2007, Frank Thomas of the Toronto Blue Jays hit his 500th career homer in the first inning of a game in Minnesota. In the ninth inning, home plate umpire Mark Wegner ejected him for arguing a called third strike. It was the first time a player had hit that milestone home run and been ejected in the same contest. As with Thomas, many ejections have come as a result of the player arguing about the balls and strikes with the arbiter, or fighting with the pitcher after being hit by a pitch. Those are less interesting than the ones we have listed here, which are presented in chronological order.

1. JACK HAYDEN

Right fielder Jack Hayden of the Boston Americans (now Red Sox) led off the game in New York on September 11, 1906, with a home run. The club eventually surrendered that lead to the Highlanders (now Yankees) as they lost, 11-3. In the bottom of the sixth inning, Frank LaPorte hit a fly to short right field that bounced between second baseman Hobe Ferris and Hayden. The ball bounced into foul territory and Hayden leisurely went after it, allowing the batter to score on the play. After the inning, as the players returned to the bench, Hayden and Ferris exchanged words about the play and then Hayden struck Ferris four times on the head. After Hayden sat down, Ferris kicked him in the mouth, loosening three teeth. Umpire Silk O'Loughlin ejected both players and the police arrested Ferris, who was released later.

2. BUCK HERZOG
Player/manager Buck Herzog of the Cincinnati Reds hit an inside-the-park home run in the top of the fifth inning in St. Louis on May 1, 1915. In the seventh frame, player/manager Miller Huggins of the Cardinals put out Tommy Leach at second base with the hidden ball trick. Herzog argued with umpire Cy Rigler about the call and was ejected. A few minutes later, Herzog returned to the field and insulted Rigler, who took off his mask and struck Herzog on the face with it. Eventually, players and policemen separated the combatants. While Rigler came out unscathed, Herzog suffered a bloody nose and black eye. Both were arrested on charges of disturbing the peace.

3. BABE RUTH
George Herman "Babe" Ruth usually was bigger than life and often out of control. On June 19, 1922, both of these traits were apparent during the Yankee game in Cleveland. In the contest won by the Indians, 4-2, Ruth hit a solo home run in the first inning to start the scoring in the game. In the eighth frame, with the New Yorkers leading, 2-1, Les Nunamaker pinch-hit for Cleveland and doubled to right. The play at second base was close and the Yankees argued with umpire Bill Dinneen. Ruth was the most vocal of the Yankees and Dinneen ejected him from the contest.

4. LOU BOUDREAU

On August 25, 1942, the Boston Red Sox won both ends of a doubleheader from Cleveland in Boston. Indians player/manager Lou Boudreau hit a solo homer to give the Tribe the lead in the top of the eleventh inning of the first game. However, in the bottom of the frame, Dom DiMaggio and Johnny Pesky both singled. Then Ted Williams forced Pesky at second, but Boudreau's throw to first was wild due to the takeout slide by Pesky. Eventually, Williams scored the winning run. During the managers meeting with the umpires before game two, Boudreau continued to protest the lack of an interference call on Pesky. He became so indignant that umpire Cal Hubbard ejected him, and also tossed Al Milnar and Otto Denning from the dugout at the same time. The Sox swept the twin bill, 4-3 and 5-1.

5. EDDIE MATHEWS

On July 2, 1961, Eddie Mathews of the Milwaukee Braves hit one home run in each game of a doubleheader against the Cincinnati Reds. In the first contest, Mathews homered in the first inning. In the top of the fourth frame, the Reds' Eddie Kasko doubled to left and, on the play, pitcher Jim O'Toole was caught in a rundown between third and home. Mathews tagged O'Toole out as the latter ran into the former at third base. After the collision and the putout, Mathews punched O'Toole and was ejected from the game.

6. DON BUFORD

Orioles left fielder Don Buford was hit by a pitch by Joel Horlen to start the second game of two in Chicago on May 31, 1971. In the third inning, Buford homered and then walked in the fifth. Buford hit a two-run homer in the sixth inning off Bart Johnson to drive in his third run and score his fourth. In the eighth frame, Johnson hit Buford with a pitch, the second time in the game that Buford had been plunked and he charged Johnson. When order was restored, Buford took first and then stole second base. The Orioles scored five runs in the ninth inning to put the game out of reach. While waiting on deck in that inning, Buford went over to the seats to warn a fan who had been yelling. A second fan attacked Buford and his teammates came to his rescue. After order was restored, Buford was ejected.

7. TED SIMMONS

The St. Louis Cardinals hosted the Chicago Cubs on May 27, 1978. Redbird catcher Ted Simmons doubled in the fourth inning, tripled in the seventh and homered in the ninth. The home run tied the game at two each, but the Cubs won in 11 innings, 3-2. Apparently Simmons and plate umpire Paul Runge were not getting along all night and, after Simmons crossed the plate on the homer, he tipped his cap to Runge and said, "Take that." The arbiter ejected Simmons for showing him up.

8. CLAUDELL WASHINGTON

On June 16, 1984, Claudell Washington of the Atlanta Braves led off the bottom of the first inning at Fulton County Stadium with a home run off Mario Soto of the Cincinnati Reds. In the third inning, Soto threw an inside pitch to Washington to push him back off the plate and send a message concerning the home run. Plate umpire Lanny Harris warned Soto, and Washington eventually struck out. Washington's next trip to the plate was in the fifth inning, and when he swung at the first pitch, his bat sailed toward Soto. As Washington went out to retrieve his bat, he and Soto exchanged words and then ran toward each other. Umpire Harris grabbed Washington but was thrown off. The benches cleared and other players tried to separate the two combatants. During the melee, Soto threw the baseball at Washington and both players were ejected. The Reds came from behind to win the contest, 2-1.

9. WILL CLARK

Will Clark played hard his whole career. On July 24, 1988, his Giants were in St. Louis playing the Cardinals. Clark smacked a three-run homer in the fifth inning to put the Giants ahead, 5-0. In the top of the eighth inning, Clark singled and was forced out at second base. He slid into Jose Oquendo, successfully breaking up the possible double play and a brawl started. Both players were ejected and then, once the game resumed, Cardinals pitcher Scott Terry threw a pitch over Mike Aldrete's head and Terry was ejected. San Francisco won the contest, 5-0.

10. RAUL CASANOVA

On August 1, 1997, at Tiger Stadium, Detroit catcher Raul Casanova hit a three-run homer in the fourth inning to give his club a 5-3 lead. In the top of the sixth, Casanova started to walk to the mound to talk with his pitcher when home plate umpire Tim McClelland told him to get back behind the plate. Apparently, the arbiter thought Casanova was stalling in order to give a relief pitcher time to warm up. McClelland ejected Casanova and Tiger manager Buddy Bell. After the game, Bell said: "To deny our catcher talking to our pitcher is something I have never seen before. That is totally unreasonable."

Don't Give Up
Your Day Job

Many players have worked other jobs during the off-season, especially before salaries rose to the high levels enjoyed by current players. Some former players have had interesting or well-known careers in other fields. Here are some of the guys who have hit at least one home run in the majors and had other well-known jobs outside of baseball.

1. DANNY AINGE

Danny Ainge played parts of three seasons from 1979 through 1981 for the Toronto Blue Jays, hitting two homers in 1979. His major league career was concurrent with his college career, in which he starred for the Brigham Young University basketball squad. Ainge won the John Wooden Award as the college basketball player of the year after his senior season. He was selected in the second round of the 1981 NBA draft by the Boston Celtics and played 14 years in the league, mostly with the Celtics. He won two World Championships out of six trips to the NBA Finals. Since retiring as a player, Ainge has worked as a television analyst, assistant coach, head coach, and is now the Executive Director of Basketball Operations with the Celtics.

2. GENE CONLEY

Gene Conley, an All-American athlete at Washington State University in 1952, pitched in the majors from 1952 through 1963. In that time, he hit five home runs and surrendered 162 while playing for the Braves (in Boston and Milwaukee), the Phillies and the Red Sox. The three-time All Star was part of the 1957 Milwaukee Braves team that won the World Series. Conley played for the Boston Celtics during the 1952–53 season and again from 1958 through 1961. Those latter squads won three consecutive NBA championships and Conley is reported to be the only person to be part of championship-winning teams in both Major League Baseball and the NBA.

3. CHUCK CONNORS

Brooklyn native Kevin Joseph Aloysius "Chuck" Connors had one at bat in 1949 for the Brooklyn Dodgers, hitting into a double play while pinch-hitting for Carl Furillo. He played in 66 games for the 1951 Chicago Cubs, hitting two home runs off New York Giants pitching at the Polo Grounds. Spending time playing for the minor league Los Angeles Angels gave him access to Hollywood and he gradually started appearing in movies and television shows. He is perhaps best known as the star of television's "The Rifleman," which ran from 1958 through 1963. Connors also played parts of two seasons (1946–48) in the NBA with the Boston Celtics. He is credited as being the first NBA player to shatter a backboard, which happened during pre-game warm-ups.

4. JOHN BERARDINO

Born Giovanni Berardino in Los Angeles and known in the baseball world as Johnny, Berardino played all or parts of 11 seasons in the major leagues from 1939 through 1952, primarily with the St. Louis Browns (now the Baltimore Orioles). He slugged 36 home runs in that time, including two in one game on June 22, 1940. Using another version of his name, John Beradino, he became a successful actor in movies and television. He was best known as Dr. Steve Hardy on the soap opera, "General Hospital," a role he played from the start of the show in 1963 through his death in 1996.

5. **BOB UECKER**

Milwaukee native Bob Uecker played parts of six years in the National League, hitting 14 home runs. Half of those four-baggers came in 1966 when he played for the Philadelphia Phillies. Uecker, who jokingly refers to himself as "Mr. Baseball," has been a radio broadcaster for the Milwaukee Brewers since 1971. He was also a frequent guest on "The Tonight Show with Johnny Carson," as well as other television shows. Uecker served as a commentator on Monday Night Baseball from 1976 through 1982, and was the star of the television show "Mr. Belvedere" from 1985 through 1990. One of his best-known movie appearances was as broadcaster Harry Doyle in "Major League." He received the Ford C. Frick Award in 2003.

6. **CARMEN FANZONE**

Carmen Fanzone made his major league debut on July 21, 1970, with the Boston Red Sox. He played ten games for Boston and was traded after the season to the Chicago Cubs. He spent four seasons with the Cubs and his first appearance for the team was a pinch-hit home run on September 8, 1971. Fanzone played 227 games and hit 20 home runs for the Cubs, while during the off-season working at his other profession as a trumpet player. He has been a successful studio musician for many years, including time with the Baja Marimba Band, and is married to singer Sue Raney.

7. BERNIE WILLIAMS

There have been two players known as Bernie Williams who have played in the majors. This one was an outfielder for the New York Yankees from 1991 through 2006, and he hit 287 regular season home runs and 22 in post season (including five in the World Series). The four-time All Star has always been interested in music and released a CD of his own music in 2003. This disc featured many of his musical friends as well as a few well-known studio musicians, including one of the top session drummers, Kenny Aronoff, who has also played for artists ranging from John Mellencamp to Joe Cocker.

8. JIM BUNNING

Hall of Fame pitcher Jim Bunning hit seven home runs during his 17-year major league career. The seven-time All Star, who surrendered 372 gopher balls, became the first pitcher to win 100 games and strike out 1,000 batters in both the National and American Leagues. Bunning went into politics after retiring from baseball, serving on the Fort Thomas City Council and in the Kentucky State Senate before being elected to the U.S. House of Representatives in 1987. Bunning is currently a U.S. Senator from Kentucky.

9. TED WILLIAMS

Teddy Ballgame hit 521 homers during his long career with the Boston Red Sox. He had two jobs outside baseball that are well documented. The first was as a U.S. Marine Corps aviator during World War II and the Korean Conflict. After he retired as a player at the end of the 1960 season, he used his skills as a hunter and fisherman as a pitchman for Sears, selling outdoor gear. Advertising featuring Williams ran all over the United States, drawing on his popularity as a ballplayer to make money for the store. In 1999, Williams was inducted into the International Game Fish Association Hall of Fame. That organization refers to Williams as "among the best of saltwater and freshwater anglers." There is one unusual tribute to Williams in Boston. The east end of the Massachusetts Turnpike is a tunnel under the Charles River leading to Logan Airport and is called the "Ted Williams Tunnel."

10. BILLY SUNDAY

Billy Sunday played eight seasons in the National League in the 1880s. Although known for his speed, he hit 12 home runs during his career as an outfielder playing for three teams. He quit baseball after the 1890 season to become an evangelist and entertained as much as preached in his campaigns, becoming a popular speaker through the end of World War I. One primary focus of his talks was prohibition.

Happy Birthday to Us!

People who share birthdays seem to have a special bond. Friendships develop because of this connection. Indeed, sometimes jokes develop about relationships that don't exist, such as calling each other "Twin." Here are some baseball twins—or at least pairs of players born on the same day (month, day, and year). These pairs are ranked by the total home runs hit by the duo, with the requirement that each of them must have hit at least career 50 dingers.

1. FRANK THOMAS AND JEFF BAGWELL

On May 27, 1968, Frank Thomas was born in Columbus, Georgia. He started his big league career in 1990 with the Chicago White Sox and has played for the Oakland Athletics and Toronto Blue Jays. Through the 2008 season, Thomas has clubbed 521 home runs. On that same day in 1968, Jeff Bagwell was born in Boston, Massachusetts. He started his big league career in 1991 and played through the 2005 season for the Houston Astros. Bagwell smashed 449 homers, giving the pair 970, the most of any pair born on the same day.

2. ALEX RODRIGUEZ AND SHEA HILLENBRAND

Alex Rodriguez, the 22nd player to hit 500 home runs, was born in New York City on July 27, 1975. He has played for the Seattle Mariners, Texas Rangers and New York Yankees, hitting 553 homers through 2008. Shea Hillenbrand was born in Mesa, Arizona on the same day and played for six different teams through 2007. Hillenbrand's 108 four-baggers gives the pair 661 combined.

3. FRED MCGRIFF AND MATT NOKES

Fred McGriff was born in Tampa, Florida on October 31, 1963—a Halloween baby! He played his first big league game in 1986 and toiled for the Toronto Blue Jays, San Diego Padres, Atlanta Braves, Tampa Bay Devil Rays, Chicago Cubs, and Los Angeles Dodgers through 2004. McGriff just missed joining the 500 Home Run Club, as he hit 493 blasts. Matt Nokes was born on Halloween, 1963 across the country in San Diego, California. He played from 1985 through 1995 for the San Francisco Giants, Detroit Tigers, New York Yankees, Baltimore Orioles, and Colorado Rockies. Nokes hit 136 homers, giving the pair a combined total of 629 four-baggers.

4. TED WILLIAMS AND BILLY JOHNSON

On August 30, 1918, Hall of Famer Ted Williams was born in San Diego, California. Williams hit 521 homers in his career with the Boston Red Sox from 1939 through 1960. On the same day across the country in Montclair, New Jersey, Billy Johnson was born. Johnson played from 1943 through 1953 with the Yankees and Cardinals and hit 61 homers. Both players had their careers interrupted by military service but combined for 582 home runs.

5. **RALPH KINER AND DEL RICE**

Ralph Kiner was born on October 27, 1922, in Santa Rita, New Mexico and played from 1946 through 1955 for the Pittsburgh Pirates, Chicago Cubs, and Cleveland Indians. Kiner smacked 369 homers and is one of the most prolific home run hitters of all time when looked at on a per-opportunity basis. On the same day that Kiner was born, Del Rice was born in Portsmouth, Ohio. Rice played from 1945 through 1961 for the Cardinals, Milwaukee Braves, Cubs, Orioles and Angels. He hit 79 dingers in that time for a combined total with Kiner of 448 home runs.

6. **CECIL COOPER AND OSCAR GAMBLE**

On December 20, 1949, Cecil Cooper was born in Brenham, Texas. He played for the Red Sox and Brewers from 1971 through 1987, hitting 241 home runs. Oscar Gamble shares a birthday with Cooper, but was born in Ramer, Alabama. Gamble played for the Cubs, Phillies, Indians, Yankees, White Sox, Padres and Rangers from 1969 through 1985 and clouted 200 home runs. The two birthday buddies combined for 441 four-baggers.

7. **RON SANTO AND DANNY CATER**

Ron Santo and Danny Cater were born on February 25, 1940, Santo in Seattle, Washington, and Cater in Austin, Texas. Santo played his entire career in Chicago from 1960 through 1974, all but the last year with the Cubs. Cater played from 1964 through 1975 for the Phillies, White Sox, Athletics (in both Kansas City and Oakland), Yankees, Red Sox, and Cardinals. Santo's 342 home runs and Cater's 66 give the pair 408 combined.

8. MICKEY TETTLETON AND MEL HALL

On September 16, 1960, Mickey Tettleton was born in Oklahoma City and Mel Hall in Lyons, New York. Tettleton played from 1984 through 1997 for the Athletics, Orioles, Tigers and Rangers while Hall played from 1981 through 1996 for the Cubs, Indians, Yankees, and Giants. Tettleton hit 245 home runs and Hall 134 for a combined total of 379.

9. RICHIE SEXSON AND EMIL BROWN

Richie Sexson was born in Portland, Oregon, on December 29, 1974. He made his big league debut in 1997 with the Indians and has played for the Brewers, Diamondbacks, Mariners, and Yankees through 2008. Chicago native Emil Brown, born the same day as Sexson in Chicago, Illinois, also debuted in 1997. He has played for the Pirates, Padres, Royals, and Athletics, hitting 59 home runs. Combined with Sexson's 306 dingers, the pair have a total of 365 four-baggers.

10. JOHN MAYBERRY AND JERRY MORALES

John Mayberry, a Detroit native, and Jerry Morales, from Yabucoa, Puerto Rico, were born on February 18, 1949. Mayberry played for the Astros, Royals, Blue Jays, and Yankees from 1968 through 1982, while Morales played for the Padres, Cubs, Cardinals, Tigers, and Mets from 1969 through 1983. Mayberry whacked 255 home runs and Morales 95 for a combined total of 350 long balls.

Who Put That There?

Here is a list of home runs that were lost due to a variety of reasons. Most of them are due to strange configurations in ballparks that stop fly balls from completing the flight over the fence. Items dangling from a ballpark roof seem to stop more homers than some pitching staffs.

1. ERNIE KRUEGER, ROBINS
On May 29, 1920, catcher Ernie Krueger of the Brooklyn Robins (now Los Angeles Dodgers) lost an inside-the-park homer when the ball rolled under the temporary stands in center field at Ebbets Field. He was awarded a ground-rule triple on the play. The hit came off Hugh McQuillan of the Boston (now Atlanta) Braves in the third inning of game two of a doubleheader.

2. JOE MEDWICK, CARDINALS
Joe Medwick lost a homer in the second game of a double-header against the Phillies in Philadelphia on June 6, 1937. He hit what would have been his tenth homer of the season in the first inning and St. Louis was leading 8-2 in the top of the fourth. An 88-minute rain delay in the first game delayed the start of game two and the 7 PM closing law was approaching.

The Phils started stalling to avoid the loss by making unnecessary pitching changes, holding mound conferences and asking for different balls. Eventually umpire Bill Klem forfeited the game to the Redbirds and all stats were wiped out because the game failed to go five innings. Phillies manager Jimmie Wilson was later fined $100 by National League president Ford Frick for his stalling tactics. Medwick was still able to win the Triple Crown that year even though he tied with Mel Ott with 31 home runs.

3. MIKE SCHMIDT, PHILLIES

On June 10, 1974, in a Phillies game at the Astrodome, Mike Schmidt hit a towering fly ball to centerfield that struck the loudspeaker 112 feet above the playing surface. It came in the first inning with two on, no one out, and he was credited with a single. The Phillies beat the Astros, 12-0.

4. WILLIE HORTON, MARINERS

Seattle's Willie Horton hit a towering fly ball in the eighth inning of a game in the Kingdome on June 5, 1979. The drive, off Detroit's John Hiller, hit a speaker in left field and was ruled a single. Without the interference, it would have been Horton's 300th home run, which came the next day off Jack Morris.

5. DAVE KINGMAN, ATHLETICS

On April 11, 1985, in the top of the sixth inning at the Kingdome, Dave Kingman hit a fly ball to left that struck a wire. The blast off Dave Geisel would have been a homer but instead was caught by Phil Bradley for the third out. So *Kingman* lost one in the *Kingdome*.

6. KEN PHELPS, MARINERS

Ken Phelps of the Mariners lost a home run to a speaker in the Kingdome on August 6, 1987. With Chuck Finley pitching for the Angels, Phelps hit a towering fly ball to center field that would have cleared the wall for a four-bagger. However, Phelps had to settle for a two-run double. Seattle won the game, 15-4.

7. CHILI DAVIS, TWINS

On July 5, 1992, in the bottom of the sixth inning at the Metrodome, Chili Davis hit a fly ball to right field off the Orioles' Rick Sutcliffe that was headed deep into the stands when it hit a speaker. The ball bounced back toward short right field where second baseman Mark McLemore made the catch for an out. The Orioles were ahead 1-0 at the time, but the Twins rallied for two runs in the bottom of the ninth for a 2-1 victory.

8. DAVID SEGUI, MARINERS

On April 8, 1998, in the Kingdome, David Segui launched a blast off Hideki Irabu of the Yankees that appeared to be his fifth home run of the season. However, the ball hit a speaker that hung 132 feet above the field in deep right-center and Segui had to settle for a triple. This hit came in the fourth inning of a game eventually won by the Yankees, 4-3.

9. JOSE CANSECO, DEVIL RAYS

Jose Canseco hit what appeared to be his eleventh homer of the season on May 2, 1999, but the ball landed on the second catwalk above left field at Tropicana Field and was ruled a double. He drove in one of the Devil Rays two runs with that fifth inning blast, but the Tigers won the game, 8-2.

10. **DAVID ORTIZ, RED SOX**

On June 15, 2006, David Ortiz hit a towering fly ball in the top of the sixth inning at the Metrodome. The ball soared toward the upper deck, but struck a speaker hanging from the ceiling and fell onto the field. Ortiz only reached first base and was out later on a double play. After the game, Boston manager Terry Francona said: "It's like playing putt-putt golf where you've got to go around the windmill. That's embarrassing. The outcome of the game should never, never hinge on a speaker." The Twins completed a three-game sweep of the Red Sox, 5-3.

The Slugger's Wife

The 1985 film *The Slugger's Wife* tells the story of the relationship between an Atlanta Braves player and a singer. The player breaks the single-season home run record after they marry, but she breaks his heart when she leaves him to go back to her career. In real (as opposed to reel) life, many players have married women who have successful careers in sports or entertainment. The women in this chapter have collected an Oscar, six Olympic Gold Medals and multiple other titles. My wife is definitely a grand slam and treats me like a Hall of Famer, so this list is for her.

1. MARILYN MONROE AND JOE DIMAGGIO

This is perhaps the most well-known pairing of a hitter and a woman who was famous in her own right. Monroe starred in many films of the 1950s and also as a pinup girl during the same time, including appearing in the first issue of *Playboy*. They were married on January 14, 1954 (after DiMaggio retired), and divorced nine months later. DiMaggio hit 361 home runs in his Hall of Fame career.

2. HALLE BERRY AND DAVID JUSTICE

Halle Berry, Miss Ohio USA 1986, won the Best Actress Oscar in 2002, and later became a "Bond Girl" in *Die Another Day*. She married David Justice of the Atlanta Braves on December 31, 1992, but they divorced in June 1997. Justice hit 305 circuit drives in his career and 14 in post-season play, including four World Series blasts.

3. MIA HAMM AND NOMAR GARCIAPARRA

Mia Hamm was a member of the Gold Medal winning U.S. women's soccer team at the 1996 and 2004 Olympic Games. She was named U.S. Soccer's Female Athlete of the Year for three consecutive years, 1994–96, and was considered to be the best woman soccer player in the world at the time. Hamm and Nomar Garciaparra married on November 22, 2003. Garciaparra, who made his debut in 1996, continues to clout homers well into the 21st century, with 226 through 2008. He hit two grand slams in the same game on May 10, 1999.

4. JULIANNE MCNAMARA AND TODD ZEILE

Julianne McNamara is another Gold Medal winning Olympic athlete. She was the first American female gymnast to win an apparatus Olympic Gold Medal when she did so at the 1984 Los Angeles games. She also won two Silver Medals at that Olympiad. In 1982, the Netherlands Flower Council, headed by namesake Dutch Queen Juliana, christened the "Julianne McNamara" rose. McNamara married Todd Zeile on January 21, 1989. Her husband hit 253 homers for 11 different teams in his big league career.

5. NANCY LOPEZ AND RAY KNIGHT

Pro golfer Nancy Lopez won the LPGA Rookie of the Year award, Player of the Year award and the Vare Trophy for lowest scoring average in 1978. She was named the Player of the

Olympic Gold Medalist Julianne McNamara competing in the 1984 Los Angeles Games. *Eileen Langsley/International Gymnast*

Year four times and is a member of the World Golf Hall of Fame. Ray Knight, former player and manager, hit 84 homers in his career. He was named the 1986 World Series Most Valuable Player.

6. MISTY MAY AND MATT TREANOR

Misty May is a Gold Medal winning beach volleyball player. She won gold at the 2004 and 2008 Summer Olympics with her long-time partner, Kerri Walsh. May was named the Most Valuable Player on the pro beach volleyball tour 2005–07. She is married to Matt Treanor, a catcher for the Florida Marlins, who has hit eight homers through 2008.

7. CINDY DOYLE AND JEFF CONINE

Cindy Doyle married Jeff Conine in 1993. They won a gold medal in the U.S. National Doubles Racquetball Championships in the 25-and-over, mixed doubles category in 1999. He is one of four sluggers to hit a pinch-hit homer in his first All Star Game at bat, accomplishing this feat in 1995, and hit 214 home runs in his career.

8. KRISTEN BABB AND ED SPRAGUE, JR.

Kristen Babb participated in the 1992 Olympics for the United States as a synchronized swimmer. She won a gold medal when the Brazilian judge mistyped the score for a competitor, Sylvie Fréchette of Canada, into the computer. The difference between the actual score (9.7) and that entered (8.7) meant that Babb won the gold instead of Fréchette. One year later, after an appeal by the Canadian Olympic federation, Fréchette was awarded her gold medal and Babb was allowed to keep hers. Babb's husband, Ed Sprague, Jr., played for the Toronto Blue Jays in 1992 and was booed by the hometown fans after the Olympics. Sprague was a member of the 1988 U.S. Olympic baseball team, which participated in the demonstration of the sport. The United States won the tournament, and the players were awarded medals that did not count in the country totals. Sprague hit 152 major league homers.

9. NANCY CHAFFEE AND RALPH KINER

Nancy Chaffee was once the world's fourth-ranked female tennis player and won three national indoor championships and two national junior championships. In the late 1940s, Chaffee played on the men's tennis team at the University of Southern California because the school did not have a women's team at the time. She was married to Ralph Kiner, who slugged 369 home runs in his career and led the National League seven consecutive seasons from 1946 through 1952.

10. ALICIA RICKTER AND MIKE PIAZZA

Alicia Rickter is an actress who later became *Playboy*'s Miss October 1995. She married All Star catcher Mike Piazza on January 29, 2005. Piazza is one of the few players to hit a major league home run at Tokyo Dome in Japan. He tied the single-season record for most parks homered in during the 2000 season by connecting in 18 different parks that year and hit 427 homers in his career.

Hey, Kid!

M ajor League players are typically in their late 20s or early 30s. However, many players have made their debut as teenagers. Tommy Brown, a part-time shortstop for the 1945 Brooklyn Dodgers made his big league debut in August 1944 at 16 years old. On August 20, 1945, he hit his first major league home run, which landed in the upper left field seats at Ebbets Field. Brown, born December 6, 1927, in Brooklyn, homered again five days later and is the only 17-year-old to hit a home run in the major leagues. After the game on August 20, the radio broadcast sponsor presented Brown with a carton of cigarettes, but they were taken from him by the Dodgers manager, Leo Durocher, who explained that Brown was too young to smoke! Here is a sample of "klouting kids" who homered before their 19th birthdays; they are in order of youngest first.

1. DANNY MURPHY

Murphy made his debut with the Chicago Cubs about two months before his 18th birthday and hit his first circuit drive on September 13, 1960, 21 days after his birthday. Murphy hit four major league homers, including two in one game in 1961. He played sparingly for three seasons with the Cubs and then returned to the majors in 1969 as a relief pitcher with the White Sox for two seasons.

2. PHIL CAVARRETTA

Cavarretta hit his first big league dinger on September 25, 1934, nine days after his debut and 68 days after his 18th birthday. He smacked 95 homers in his 22-year career, including four as a pinch hitter and four as an 18-year-old. He played his entire career in his native Chicago, 20 seasons with the Cubs and two with the White Sox. Cavarretta hit the fourth most career homers as a teenager with 14.

3. MEL OTT

Hall of Famer Mel Ott struck 511 major league home runs in 22 years with the New York (now San Francisco) Giants. His first came on July 18, 1927, at the Polo Grounds in New York four months after his 18th birthday. Ott hit 323 four-baggers at the Polo Grounds, the most homers by one player at one park in history. He accomplished this by taking aim at the right field corner, where the distance from home plate to the right field pole was only 258 feet. Ott hit the second-most career homers as a teenager, with 19.

4. ED KRANEPOOL

New York native Ed Kranepool played his entire 18-year career with the Mets. After making his debut on September 22, 1962, he whacked his first homer the next April 19th. Kranepool hit 12 of his 118 circuit drives as a teenager, which places him sixth on the all-time teenager list. Two of those came before his 19th birthday. On August 14, 1964, Kranepool hit two homers off Rick Wise, who was also a teenager. This is the only instance of a teenager slugging two homers in one game off another teenager.

5. LEW BROWN

Lew Brown made his debut with the Boston Red Caps (now the Atlanta Braves) in 1876. The 18-year-old Massachusetts native hit the first of his ten big league homers on July 20, 1876. He played for six different teams through the 1884 season and hit two home runs as an 18-year-old.

6. WAYNE CAUSEY

Wayne Causey hit his first major league homer on June 17, 1955, six months after his 18th birthday and 12 days after his major league debut. An infielder, he started his career with the Baltimore Orioles and played for four other teams in a career in which he hit 35 home runs.

7. LEW MALONE

Lew Malone, who played 133 games from 1915 through 1919, hit exactly one home run in his career. That came on September 3, 1915, for the Philadelphia (now Oakland) Athletics, just six months after his 18th birthday. The Baltimore native also played for the Brooklyn Dodgers.

8. SCOTT STRATTON

Pitcher Scott Stratton played in the majors from 1888 through 1895, mostly in Louisville, Kentucky, which was then a major league city. He whacked eight four-baggers in his career, at a time when players did not hit many homers. The first of his circuit clouts came on April 21, 1888, in the fourth inning of his first big league game.

9. MONTE WARD

Hall of Famer John Montgomery Ward played 17 years from 1878 through 1894. In his career, he was primarily a middle infielder and pitcher. The first of his 26 homers came on

September 27, 1878, for the National League's Providence Grays, about seven months after he turned 18.

10. ROBIN YOUNT
Robin Yount hit 11 of his 251 home runs as a teenager, including three before his 19th birthday. The first of these came on April 13, 1974, in his sixth game in the big leagues. Yount, who played his entire career with the Brewers, played in three All Star Games and was elected to the Hall of Fame in 1999.

Hello, My Name is . . .

The most prolific family name for home runs in history is Williams. Collectively, 28 different players named Williams have clouted 2,613 homers through 2008. Second place belongs to the Johnsons, who have hit 2,101 four-baggers. Here is a sample of the slugging Williamses.

1. **TED, 521**

Ted Williams played his entire 19-year career with the Boston Red Sox. He was the fourth batter (and still the oldest) to hit 500 homers and led the American League four times in home runs. The two-time AL Most Valuable Player was elected to the Hall of Fame in 1966.

2. **BILLY, 426**

Hall of Famer Billy Williams hit most of his clouts for the Chicago Cubs but ended his career with the Oakland Athletics. He was selected as the 1961 National League Rookie of the Year and played in six All Star games.

3. **MATT, 378**

Three people named Matt Williams have played in the majors but only one of them homered. This Matt played for the San

Francisco Giants, Cleveland Indians, and Arizona Diamond-backs from 1987 through 2003. Matt holds the distinction of being the only player to hit home runs in the World Series in three different decades for three different teams.

4. BERNIE AND BERNIE, 291
Two players named Bernie Williams have played in the big leagues. The first played for the San Francisco Giants in the early 1970s and hit four homers. The second played for the New York Yankees from 1991 through 2006 and smacked 287 regular season home runs, five in the World Series and 22 total in post-season play.

5. CY, 251
Fred "Cy" Williams toiled in the National League for the Cubs and Phillies from 1912 through 1930, leading the league four times in those seasons. When he retired, Cy was third on the all-time home run list behind Babe Ruth (who had hit 565 at that time) and Rogers Hornsby (who had hit 279).

6. KEN AND KEN, 223
There have been two players named Ken Williams who have homered in the majors. The first played from 1915 through 1929 and clobbered 196 home runs. He led the American League in 1922 with 39. The second Ken played from 1986 through 1991 and hit 27 four-baggers. He later became the general manager of the White Sox.

7. EARL, 138
The name Earl Williams applies to two former big leaguers, only one of whom homered. He was the 1971 National League Rookie of the Year and played through most of the 1970s for four teams.

8. GERALD, 85

Gerald started his career with the Yankees and played for five other teams from 1992 through 2005, including both the Yankees and the Mets in New York. During his two stints with the Yankees, he was a teammate of Bernie Williams.

9. DICK, 70

Dick Williams hit 70 home runs as a part-time player from 1951 through 1964, playing for five teams. However, he is better known as a World Series winning manager, as he took three different teams to the Series, winning twice with Oakland. He was inducted into the Hall of Fame in 2008.

10. JIMMY, 49

Jimmy Williams played from 1899 through 1909 and hit 49 homers at a time when home runs were not common. There was also a Jim and a Jimy Williams who played in the majors, but neither homered.

Island Hoppers

The 17,000 people who have played in the major leagues since the 19th century have been born in many countries, with the great majority from the United States (over 15,000). However, there have been players born in Belgium, France, the Canal Zone, and the Netherlands. Otto Hess, who hit five homers while pitching for the Cleveland Indians and Boston Braves in the early part of the 20th century, is the only player born in Switzerland. Danny Graves, who hit two homers while pitching for the Cincinnati Reds at the beginning of the 21st century, was born in South Vietnam in 1973. Here is a list of the top home run hitters from ten island countries, listed in alphabetical order.

1. ARUBA

There have been four major league players who were born on the island of Aruba, which is located off the coast of Venezuela. The first of these players was Eugene Kingsale, who played for the Baltimore Orioles starting in September 1996. Kingsale hit three big league homers in his career, the only homers hit by an Aruban. Five days after Kingsale's debut, Calvin Maduro played his first big league game. The other two players from Aruba are Radhames Dykhoff, who played one game in 1998, and pitcher Sidney Ponson.

2. BAHAMAS

The Bahamas have produced five big league players, the first being Andre Rodgers, who played from 1957 through 1967 and hit 45 home runs. Rodgers, who was born in Nassau, played for the Giants, Cubs, and Pirates. The last player born in the island nation off the coast of Florida was Wil Culmer, who played seven games for the 1983 Cleveland Indians, hitting no homers. The other three natives of the Bahamas are Tony Curry, who hit six homers, Ed Armbrister, who hit four and pitcher Wenty Ford, who surrendered three but hit none.

3. CUBA

Cuba, an island about 90 miles south of Florida, has produced many major league players through the years. The first was Steve Bellan, who played briefly in the 19th century. The Cuban native who hit the most major league home runs is Rafael Palmeiro, who was born in Havana in 1964 and whacked 569 homers during his 20-year career. He is one of four batters with 500 homers and 3,000 hits, the others being Willie Mays, Hank Aaron, and Eddie Murray. Two other Cuban natives have hit at least 300 major league home runs: Jose Canseco (462) and Tony Perez (379).

4. CURACAO

Curacao, also known as the Netherlands Antilles, is located off the coast of Venezuela, likes its neighbor, Aruba. Ten major league players have come from Curacao, starting with Hensley Meulens, who made his debut in August 1989. Andruw Jones has hit 371 four-baggers to lead the island in home run production. Jones hit a home run in each of his first two at bats in the World Series in 1996 to become the second player in history to perform that feat, after Gene Tenace.

5. DOMINICAN REPUBLIC
The Dominican Republic, which occupies more than half of the island of Hispaniola in the Caribbean, has produced many major-league ball players. In fact, it has the second highest total of any country, trailing only the United States , with nearly 500 natives who have played in the majors. The first player to come off the island and make it to the major leagues was Ozzie Virgil, Sr. in 1956. He was followed shortly thereafter by Felipe Alou and many others. The most prolific home run slugger from the Dominican Republic is Sammy Sosa, who was born in San Pedro de Macoris, a hotbed of players. Sosa hit his 600th homer on June 20, 2007, only the fifth player to attain that milestone, and hit 609 four-baggers in his career. Only one other Dominican native has hit 400 dingers: Manny Ramirez, with 527 through 2008.

6. IRELAND
Many 19th century major leaguers were born in Ireland, part of the large number of immigrants to the United States in the middle of that century. The last player born in Ireland was Joe Cleary, who pitched to nine batters in one game for the Washington Senators in 1945. Jack Doyle, a native of Killorgin, played in the majors from 1889 through 1905 and hit 25 home runs. He also managed 81 big league games and umpired 42 games, quite a trio of jobs.

7. JAMAICA
Another island in the Caribbean, Jamaica, has produced three major leaguers. The first and most prolific home run hitter,

Charles "Chili" Davis, was born in Kingston. The switch-hitting outfielder smacked 350 home runs in his career while playing for five teams in both leagues. Devon White, also from Kingston, was a Gold Glove winning outfielder who hit 208 home runs. The third Jamaican to play in the big leagues was Rolando Roomes, who hit nine homers in the late 1980s in the National League.

8. PUERTO RICO

Puerto Rico has been a major spawning ground of ballplayers for many years, starting with Hiram Bithorn in 1942. More big-time sluggers have come from this island than any of the others listed here, with four who have hit 300 career homers. The leader is Carlos Delgado, who has hit 469 big flies through 2008. During that season, he passed Juan Gonzalez, who hit 434 in his 17-year big league career. Hall of Famer Orlando Cepeda (379 homers) and Ruben Sierra (306 homers) are the other two Puerto Rico natives with at least 300 four-baggers.

9. TAIWAN

The first major league player born on the island of Taiwan debuted in September 2002. Chin-Feng Chen, born in Tainan City, hit no homers in a three-year major league career. Other players from Taiwan are Chin-hui Tsao, Chien-Ming Wang, Hong-Chih Kuo, and Chin-lung Hu. Kuo hit the first home run by a Taiwanese player on June 12, 2007, but Hu smacked two in September that year to acquire the lead for his island nation. Of course, every time Hu singles, he answers the old question: "Who's on first?"

10. VIRGIN ISLANDS

Eleven players from the Virgin Islands have played in the major leagues, starting with Joe Christopher in 1959. Christopher, who was born in Frederiksted, St. Croix, hit 29 home runs in his career as an outfielder. However, the player from the Virgin Islands with the most home runs is Elrod Hendricks, who was born in Charlotte Amalie, St. Thomas. Hendricks, who wore the uniform of the Baltimore Orioles as a player and coach longer than any other person, hit 62 major league homers. He served as the Orioles bullpen coach from 1978 until his death after the 2005 season.

The Most Homer–
Happy Teams

Since 1998, there have been 30 major league baseball teams but this has not always been the case, as many of them have been in existence for less than 50 years. However, some of the long-time franchises have clubbed well over 11,000 four-baggers in their time. Here are the teams with the most home runs through the 2008 season.

1. NEW YORK YANKEES
This team has earned the nickname "The Bronx Bombers" through nearly constant slugging through the decades. Since moving from Baltimore to New York for the 1903 season, the Yankees have slugged, swatted and belted 13,803 four-baggers. They hit 57 during their two-year existence as the Baltimore Orioles, giving them a franchise total of 13,860. Babe Ruth is the team leader with 659 homers hit for the Yankees.

2. SAN FRANCISCO GIANTS
The Giants played from 1883 through 1957 in New York City and moved to California for the 1958 season. While in the Empire State, they hit 5,775 home runs and since their move to the West Coast they have hit 7,465 homers. That gives them the second-highest franchise total and top National

League total of 13,240. Willie Mays hit 646 home runs for the Giants, with 187 for New York and 459 for San Francisco.

3. CHICAGO CUBS
Although they have used many nicknames through the years, the Cubs have always played in Chicago. Since 1916, they have played at Wrigley Field, a park that can be conducive to home run hitting. They have the third-highest franchise home run total of 12,435 since 1876, and Sammy Sosa is the franchise leader with 545 four baggers.

4. ATLANTA BRAVES
The Braves have played continuously since the start of the National League in 1876. However, they have called three cities home in that time as they played in Boston until 1952 (hitting 3,424 home runs in that time) and in Milwaukee from 1953 through 1965 (hitting 2,230). Atlanta has been home since 1966 and they have hit 6,521 homers since moving to Georgia, giving them a franchise total of 12,175. The record for one batter is the 733 home runs hit by Hank Aaron for Milwaukee and Atlanta.

5. DETROIT TIGERS
The Tigers were a charter member of the American League when the league formed in 1901 and always have played in Detroit. For many years, they played in a homer-friendly park that went by many names, the last being Tiger Stadium but now they play in a more pitcher-friendly home, Comerica Park. The Tigers have hit 12,011 home runs since 1901 and the individual leader is Al Kaline with 399.

6. BOSTON RED SOX
Like the Tigers, the Red Sox are a charter member of the American League and have spent most of their time in a

homer-friendly ballpark, Fenway Park. The Boston Red Sox have hit 11,630 four-baggers since 1901 and Ted Williams hit 521 of them to lead the team all-time.

7. CINCINNATI REDS
The Reds started play in 1882 in the American Association and joined the National League in 1890. They have slugged 11,496 home runs since 1882, including 11,229 in the NL, and Hall of Famer Johnny Bench has led the way with 389 for the Reds.

8. PHILADELPHIA PHILLIES
The Phillies have been a member of the National League since 1883 and, in that time, they have hit 11,407 homers. Mike Schmidt hit 548 home runs for the club, the most of any single batter in franchise history.

9. OAKLAND ATHLETICS
The Athletics have played in three cities since helping found the American League in 1901. They played in Philadelphia through the 1954 season, hitting 3,502 during that time. From 1955 through 1967, they played in Kansas City and hit 1,480 in the Midwest. Since 1968, they have called Oakland home and have hit 6,407 homers on the West Coast, for a franchise total of 11,389. Mark McGwire homered 363 times for the Oakland Athletics to set the franchise record.

10. CLEVELAND INDIANS
The Indians, another charter team in the American League, have played their home games in Cleveland in a number of ballparks. Since 1901, they have slugged 11,300 home runs. Jim Thome hit 334 for the Tribe to top the individual list for the franchise.

Ten Times Ten

Most people are interested in round numbers like 10, 100, 1000. Why is ten better than nine or 11? Maybe it is because we have ten fingers or (more likely) because we use a ten-based counting system. Here are the home run leaders for each of the last ten decades.

1. **2000–2008: ALEX RODRIGUEZ**
Alex Rodriguez has become one of the best players in the game in the first decade of the 21st century. Through the 2008 season, ARod has hit 405 homers for three American League teams in this decade, including six years over 40 and three with 50. The twelve-time All Star led the AL in home runs five times in seven years from 2001 through 2007.

2. **1990–99: MARK MCGWIRE**
Mark McGwire hit 405 homers in the ten-year span of the 1990s. In 1996, he led the American League (and the majors) with 52 home runs. In 1997, he hit 58 homers to lead the majors. The next year, McGwire broke Roger Maris's single-season record by slugging 70 homers. Big Mac led the majors again in 1999 with 65 home runs. The 245 home runs he

slugged from 1996 through 1999 are the most for any single player for four consecutive seasons.

3. 1980–89: MIKE SCHMIDT
Mike Schmidt, who played his entire career with the Philadelphia Phillies, hit 313 of his 548 home runs in the 1980s. Having led the National League in homers three times in the 1970s, Schmidt topped the circuit five times in the 1980s (1980, 1981, 1983, 1984, and 1986). Schmidt won the NL Most Valuable Player Award and the World Series Most Valuable Player Award in 1980 and then won the NL MVP again in 1981 and 1986.

4. 1970–79: WILLIE STARGELL
Willie Stargell, known as "Pops" later in his career, hit 296 dingers in the 1970s while playing for the Pittsburgh Pirates. He led the National League in homers in both 1971 and 1973 but had his best year in 1979, when he won the NL Most Valuable Player Award and the same award for the National League Championship Series and the World Series. He finished his Hall of Fame career with 475 four-baggers.

5. 1960–69: HARMON KILLEBREW
Harmon Killebrew was the slugging champion of the 1960s, as he smacked 393 homers during that period. "The Killer" played most of his career with the Minnesota Twins franchise, which was known as the Washington Senators through 1960. Killebrew led the American League in homers in 1959 as a Senator and then led the AL as a Twin from 1962 through 1964, and again in 1967 (tied with Carl Yastrzemski) and 1969. Killebrew was the American League Most Valuable Player in 1969.

6. 1950–59: DUKE SNIDER

Edwin Donald Snider, "The Duke of Flatbush," hit 407 home runs in his career, with 326 of those during the 1950s. Los Angeles native Snider spent most of his career with the Dodgers, both in Brooklyn and Los Angeles. His 43 four-baggers in 1956 led the National League one year after Brooklyn beat the New York Yankees in the World Series.

7. 1940–49: TED WILLIAMS

Boston Red Sox slugger Ted Williams might have led the league in nicknames during his time in the majors. One of those appellations, "The Thumper," correctly names him as one of the premier sluggers of his day. Williams hit 234 of his 521 homers during the 1940s to lead the majors. This feat is impressive since he missed three complete seasons from 1943 through 1945 while serving in the U.S. Marine Corps as an aviator. Ted led the American League in bombs in 1941, 1942, 1947, and 1949. He won the AL Most Valuable Player Award in 1946 and 1949.

8. 1930–39: JIMMIE FOXX

Jimmie Foxx, called "The Beast," hit 534 homers in his career, most of them for the Philadelphia Athletics and Boston Red Sox. During the 1930s, Foxx slugged 415 home runs, leading the American League in 1932, 1933, 1935, and 1939. He won the league's Most Valuable Player Award in 1932, 1933, and 1938. Foxx never hit fewer than 30 homers in a season during the decade, including two years with at least 50. He was the first batter to hit at least 200 homers for each of two teams, with 302 for the Athletics and 222 for the Red Sox.

The statue of Jimmie Foxx in his home town of Sudlersville,
Maryland. *Photo by the author*

9. **1920–29: BABE RUTH**

It might take an entire book to describe fully the career of George Herman "Babe" Ruth. He redefined the game of baseball in the early 1920s with his slugging exploits, after having been a star pitcher in the previous decade. Ruth swatted 467 of his 714 home runs during the 1920s. Having led the American League in homers in 1918 and 1919, he led the circuit eight times out of ten in the 1920s and then twice more in the 1930s. He broke the single-season record four times from 1919 through 1927 and is the only player to break his own record. Eighty years later, sluggers still try to emulate the Bambino, but few players come close to his greatness.

10. **1910–19: GAVVY CRAVATH**

Clifford "Gavvy" Cravath hit 116 home runs during the second decade of the 20th century, all but three of his career total. Playing for the Philadelphia Phillies, he led the National League in six of seven consecutive years from 1913 through 1919, finishing third in 1916. Playing at Baker Bowl in Philadelphia, which featured a short right field line, Cravath hit 92 of 116 homers at home as a Phillie, even though he was a right-handed hitter.

Initially, I Thought It Was . . .

People have played in the major leagues with last names starting with 25 of the 26 letters of the alphabet, as there has never been a player whose last name started with "X." There are 13 letters through 2008 whose leader hit at least 500 homers; for example, Willie Mays and his 660 dingers tops the list of players whose last name starts with "M." At the other end of the spectrum, this list shows the ten initials with the lowest career totals for the individual leader.

1. CARLOS QUENTIN, 50

The only letter without a player who has hit 100 home runs is "Q." Carlos Quentin made his debut in July 2006 and, through 2008, he has slugged 50 homers for the Diamondbacks and White Sox. If his total is added to that of the second place "Q" guy (Mark Quinn with 45), they still do not reach 100. Quinn played parts of four seasons with the Royals.

2. CHASE UTLEY, 130

Chase Utley has played for the Phillies since 2003 and hit 130 four-baggers. In 2008, Utley passed Willie Upshaw for the lead on the "U" list. Upshaw played most of his career with the

Blue Jays, hitting 123 homers. The only other player with a "U" initial to smack 100 homers was Juan Uribe with 111.

3. **PETE INCAVIGLIA, 206**

Pete Incaviglia hit 206 home runs in his 12-year major league career with his highest season total coming his rookie year, as he hit 30 in 1986 for the Texas Rangers. He played in Japan during the 1995 season, but returned for three more seasons to complete his career. Inky was born in a community better known for golf than baseball, Pebble Beach, California. Raul Ibanez has hit 182 long balls through the 2008 season and seems poised to pass Incaviglia.

4. **TODD ZEILE, 253**

Three sluggers whose last name starts with the last letter of the alphabet each have hit at least 200 major league home runs. Todd Zeile is the career leader with 253, while Gus Zernial (237) and Richie Zisk (207) have also topped the 200 milestone. Zernial played outfield for three American League squads from 1949 through 1959. He hit 42 homers in 1953 and at least 30 in two others seasons. Zisk toiled for 13 years in the majors with 30 homers in 1977 and 20 or more in four other seasons. Zeile played in the majors from 1989 through 2004 and his 253 homers came through a steady pace as Zeile never hit more than 31 in any one season.

5. **GREG LUZINSKI, 307**

Greg Luzinski played in the majors from 1970 through 1984, primarily for the Phillies. He was one of the premiere sluggers of the 1970s, as he had the tenth best total for the decade. The only other "L" player who hit 300 homers is Fred Lynn, who ended his career with one less four-bagger than Luzinski.

Lynn was the American League's Rookie of the Year and Most Valuable Player in 1975.

6. GREG VAUGHN, 355

Two players with a last name starting with "V" hit 300 homers—and they have the same last name! Greg Vaughn, who played from 1989 through 2003, hit 355 home runs for five teams in both leagues. In 1997, he hit 41 homers while being traded from the Brewers to the Padres. His cousin, Mo Vaughn, smacked 328 home runs in his career, primarily for the Red Sox. Mo was the American League Most Valuable Player in 1995 and both Vaughns are two-time All Stars.

7. FRANK HOWARD, 382

Frank "Hondo" Howard, all 6'7" of him, crushed 382 major league home runs and led the American League in that category twice with 44. In the late 1960s, as a member of the Washington Senators, he was called the "Capital Punisher" for his mighty blasts at RFK Stadium, which was not conducive to hitting home runs. Gil Hodges hit 370 homers for the Dodgers (in Brooklyn and Los Angeles) and the New York Mets.

8. GRAIG NETTLES, 390

Graig Nettles far surpassed any other home run hitter whose last name starts with "N" as Bill Nicholson holds the second place spot with 235. Nettles played most of his career with the Yankees but he also toiled for five other clubs. His brother, Jim, is not quite so high on the homer list, having hit 16 in his short career. Graig is known for his glove work around third base, having turned in many fine plays in five World Series. He hit 40 home runs after turning 40 years old, the ninth highest total for that feat.

9. **DARRELL EVANS, 414**

Darrell Evans hit 60 of his 414 career homers after his 40th birthday, the third highest total in that category. Evans hit at least 30 homers in a season for three different teams: the Braves, the Giants and the Tigers. He is one of three players to hit at least 100 career homers for three teams, along with Reggie Jackson and Alex Rodriguez.

10. **JOSE CANSECO, 462**

Jose Canseco played in the majors for seven teams from 1985 through 2001. He led the American League twice, with 42 in 1988 and 44 in 1991. He was the AL Rookie of the Year in 1986 and it's MVP in 1988. He slugged three World Series homers with the Athletics. Jose's twin brother, Ozzie, played 24 games in the major leagues but hit no home runs.

We Cover the Field (Career Edition)

The rulebook states that baseball is a game played by two teams of nine players each. That is certainly true in the National League but the American League has played with a tenth person in the lineup since 1973, a designated hitter. This list contains the ten players who have hit the most home runs in a career at those ten positions. Maybe that makes this our starting lineup for the All-Time Home Run Team. By the way, the career leader in pinch-hit home runs is Cliff Johnson, who whacked 20 home runs while hitting for someone else.

1. WES FERRELL, PITCHER

Wes Ferrell pitched for six teams from 1927 through 1941 with most of his career spent playing for the Indians and Red Sox. He surrendered 132 homers on the mound but hit 37 as a pitcher during his career. Ferrell also clouted a pinch-hit homer on July 21, 1935, when he hit for Boston teammate Lefty Grove. Two other hurlers, Warren Spahn and Bob Lemon, each hit 35 home runs in their careers.

2. MIKE PIAZZA, CATCHER

On May 5, 2004, Mike Piazza hit his 352nd home run as a catcher to pass Carlton Fisk as the all-time leader for backstops. Through the 2007 season, Piazza smacked 396 four-baggers as a catcher, thus extending his record. The 1993 National League Rookie of the Year and 1996 All Star Game Most Valuable Player joined the 400 Homer Club in 2006 finishing his career with 427 total homers.

3. MARK MCGWIRE, FIRST BASE

Mark McGwire, who held the single-season home run record for three years, hit 583 circuit drives in his career. McGwire played for the Athletics and Cardinals and hit 566 homers as a first baseman, breaking the record of 493 by Lou Gehrig on September 1, 1999. McGwire, who was the 1987 American League Rookie of the Year, hit more than 60 homers in two seasons, 1998 and 1999.

4. JEFF KENT, SECOND BASE

Rogers Hornsby held the record for second base for many years with 265 homers. Fellow Hall of Famer Joe Morgan hit 266 at the Keystone Sack to pass Hornsby in 1984, and was in turn passed by Ryne Sandberg in 1997. Jeff Kent, who has played most of his career with the Mets and Giants, grabbed the record for himself on October 2, 2004, with his last home run of the season. Through 2008, the 2000 National League Most Valuable Player has smacked 351 homers as a second baseman.

5. MIKE SCHMIDT, THIRD BASE

Three-time National League Most Valuable Player Mike Schmidt is considered by many baseball people to be the best third baseman of all time. He was great with the glove (ten Gold Gloves) *and* the bat. Schmidt led the National League in homers eight times and topped Eddie Mathews as the most prolific home run hitter at the Hot Corner on September 20,

1987, when he hit his 487th circuit clout as a third baseman. Schmidt, who was elected to the Hall of Fame in 1995, hit 509 of his 548 homers as a third sacker.

6. CAL RIPKEN, SHORTSTOP
Cal Ripken, voted into the Hall of Fame in 2007, played most of his career at shortstop before moving to third base late in his career. Voted the American League Rookie of the Year in 1982, he won the AL Most Valuable Player Award in 1983 and 1991. Ripken was an 18-time All Star and won the game's Most Valuable Player Award in 1991 and 2001. On July 15, 1993, Ripken hit home run number 278 as a shortstop to pass Ernie Banks and ended his career with 345 homers at shortstop. Through the 2008 season, Ripken is one ahead of Alex Rodriguez, who has been playing third base since joining the Yankees in 2004.

7. BARRY BONDS, LEFT FIELD
Barry Bonds set the single-season home run record in 2001 when he smashed 73 four-baggers. He ended the 2007 season with 725 homers as a left fielder, extending his own record that he established by passing Ted Williams on April 26, 2001. Ted Williams hit 477 of his 521 career home runs as a left fielder. Babe Ruth hit 313 homers as a left fielder and was the leader when he retired in 1935. Ralph Kiner and Luis Gonzalez have also passed Ruth on this list.

8. WILLIE MAYS, CENTER FIELD
The "Say Hey Kid" was one of three celebrated center fielders in New York City during the 1950s and they all place in the top five center fielder sluggers of all time. Willie hit 640 homers as a middle outfielder, Mickey Mantle hit 432 and Duke Snider 356 as center fielders, completing the New York trio.

Ken Griffey, Jr. has hit 542 homers as a center fielder through 2008. During the 2008 season, Jim Edmonds passed Snider to move into fourth place on this list, while Andruw Jones ended the season tied with Snider.

9. SAMMY SOSA, RIGHT FIELD

Slammin' Sammy Sosa hit 538 homers as a right fielder. Sosa has played most of his career with the Chicago Cubs, although he has played with three other teams. Sosa, the 1998 National League Most Valuable Player, passed Hank Aaron on the right fielders list on April 15, 2005, when he slugged his 528th at that position. Babe Ruth swatted 354 home runs as a right fielder in his career and, when he retired, he was the career leader in both left and right fields. He is now fifth in left field and sixth in right field.

10. FRANK THOMAS, DESIGNATED HITTER

Frank Thomas became the all-time leader for most home runs hit as a designated hitter on June 17, 2007, while playing for the Toronto Blue Jays. That day, he smacked his 244th homer as a DH in an inter-league game against the Washington Nationals, passing Edgar Martinez on the list. Martinez had passed Harold Baines in 2004. Thomas has played most of his career with the White Sox and was named American League Most Valuable Player in 1993 and 1994. Through 2008, he had hit 269 homers as a designated hitter. In 2008, David Ortiz moved past Martinez into second place on this list with 248 homers as a designated hitter.

We Cover the Field (Single-Season Edition)

The following ten players are the single-season home run leaders at each fielding position and at designated hitter. Four of the guys on this list are also the career leaders at that position: Ferrell, McGwire, Bonds, and Sosa. The single-season record for most homers as a pinch hitter is seven, held by Dave Hansen of the Los Angeles Dodgers (2000) and Craig Wilson of the Pittsburgh Pirates (2001).

1. WES FERRELL, PITCHER

Wes Ferrell, who hit the most career homers as a hurler, smacked nine during the 1931 season for the Cleveland Indians. He is also tied for the second-highest total with the seven he hit in 1933. Other pitchers who hit seven in one season are: Jack Stivetts (1890), Bob Lemon (1949), Don Newcombe (1955), Don Drysdale (1958 and 1965), Earl Wilson (1968), and Mike Hampton (2001).

2. JAVY LOPEZ, CATCHER

Javy Lopez caught for the Atlanta Braves for 12 years before playing for the Orioles and briefly for the Red Sox. In 2003, Lopez hit 42 of his 43 homers as a catcher, thus breaking the record for backstops of Todd Hundley. Hundley set his mark with 41 home runs in 1996, breaking the long-time record of Roy Campanella, who smashed 40 in 1953.

3. **MARK MCGWIRE, FIRST BASE**
McGwire is the second player on this list who also holds the career title for the same position. In 1998, when Big Mac set the single-season record with 70 four-baggers, 69 of them came as a first baseman. The previous record was set in 1938 when Hank Greenberg hit 58 home runs as a first sacker. McGwire hit at least 50 homers as a first baseman three times; Jimmie Foxx (twice), Johnny Mize, and Ryan Howard have also hit at least 50 homers in one season as a first baseman.

4. **ROGERS HORNSBY AND DAVEY JOHNSON, SECOND BASE**
Rogers Hornsby was the first National Leaguer to hit at least 40 homers in one year when he smacked 42 to lead the majors in 1922. He also held the National League career record from 1929 through 1937 with the 298 he hit in the Senior Circuit. Davey Johnson matched Hornsby's single-season total as a second baseman in 1973, when he led a trio of Atlanta Braves who each hit 40 four-baggers that season. The only other player to hit at least 40 homers as a second baseman was Ryne Sandberg in 1990, who hit exactly 40.

5. **ALEX RODRIGUEZ, THIRD BASE**
Alex Rodriguez hit 52 of his 54 homers in 2007 as a third baseman, thus breaking the record of 48 at that position held jointly by Mike Schmidt (1980) and Adrian Beltre (2004). Schmidt had broken the mark of Eddie Mathews, who slugged 47 homers in 1953. Check the next item on this list for more ARod.

6. **ALEX RODRIGUEZ, SHORTSTOP**

In 1958, Ernie Banks hit 47 homers as a shortstop. Banks had hit 44 in 1955 to beat the 1949 record of Vern Stephens, who hit 39. Banks also hit 45 in 1959 and 41 in 1960. Alex Rodriguez has hit 40 homers as a shortstop six times, with his highest total the 57 he hit in 2002. Banks and Rodriguez hold the ten top spots on the all-time list for most homers in a season by a shortstop. ARod has the highest single-season total at shortstop *and* third base, which is quite a feat.

7. **BARRY BONDS, LEFT FIELD**

In 2001, when Barry Bonds hit 73 home runs, 71 of them came as a left fielder. The previous record holder, Ralph Kiner, had hit 51 in 1947 and 54 in 1949. Kiner had topped the record of Babe Ruth, who swatted 51 four-baggers in 1921 as a left fielder. In 2001, Luis Gonzalez also beat Kiner's record by clouting 57. Bonds is another who leads both for a season and a career at one position.

8. **HACK WILSON AND KEN GRIFFEY, JR., CENTER FIELD**

Hack Wilson held the National League single-season record from 1930 through 1998. The 56 Wilson hit in 1930 is still the record for a center fielder in a season. Wilson, who was elected to the Hall of Fame in 1979, had his best years with the Cubs, although he also played with the New York (now San Francisco) Giants, Brooklyn (now Los Angeles) Dodgers, and Philadelphia Phillies. Ken Griffey, Jr. tied Wilson's record in 1998, the season after being named the American League's Most Valuable Player.

9. **SAMMY SOSA, RIGHT FIELD**

In 1961, Roger Maris hit 61 home runs to set a new single-season record. Maris played most of the season in right field for the Yankees, hitting 56 of his blasts at that position. The previous mark had been 42, hit by Mel Ott in 1929 and Rocky Colavito in 1959. In 1998, Sammy Sosa hit 65 homers while patrolling the right garden, thus now holding both the season and career marks for right fielders.

10. DAVID ORTIZ, DESIGNATED HITTER

The designated hitter has been part of American League games since 1973. Through the 2004 season, 19 players had hit 30 or more homers as a designated hitter. However, the first DH to smash 40 homers was David Ortiz, who hit 43 in 2005 and upped the record with 47 in 2006. Ortiz broke the record held jointly by Rafael Palmeiro (1999) and Edgar Martinez (2000), who each hit 37 homers. In 2006, three designated hitters whacked 39 homers each: Frank Thomas, Jim Thome and Travis Hafner, but Ortiz remains the only DH to hit 40 in one season.

First Time Ever
I Saw Your Place

Starting with the opening of Baltimore's Oriole Park at Camden Yards in 1992, there has been a boom in the building business. Seventeen of the thirty major league teams play in ballparks that opened after Camden Yards and an 18th, Dolphin Stadium, was not used for baseball until 1993 when the Marlins came into existence. Most of these new homes favor hitters and this has been one of the primary reasons for the hitting and home run surge that started in the mid-1990s. Here are the ten parks that have opened since 2000 and the batter who struck the first four-bagger at the park.

1. MINUTE MAID PARK, HOUSTON

On April 7, 2000, the Astros played their first game in their new home. It was called Enron Field at the time under a licensing agreement between the club and the company by the same name. After the collapse of Enron, the Astros changed the name to Astros Field for the start of the 2002 season and then announced a new agreement to name the field Minute Maid Park, which took effect on June 5, 2002. Philadelphia Phillies third baseman Scott Rolen led off the top of the seventh inning of the first game with the park's first homer. Richard Hidalgo hit the first Astros homer in the bottom of the frame for the only Astros run in a 4-1 loss by the home team. The field has a retractable roof in case of inclement weather.

2. AT&T PARK, SAN FRANCISCO

Four days after Houston inaugurated their new stadium, the San Francisco Giants played their first contest at Pacific Bell Park on April 11, 2000. The park features a look at San Francisco Bay beyond the right field wall into which many home run balls fly. Kevin Elster of the Los Angeles Dodgers hit a solo homer in the top of the third frame of the first game, which he followed with two more in the fifth and eighth innings. Thus, Elster hit the first homer and had the first multi-homer game at the new park. In the bottom of the third, Barry Bonds, who has hit more homers at the park than any other hitter, clobbered the first circuit drive by a Giant at the park. Like Enron, Pac Bell Park has seen two name changes: to SBC Park in 2004 and to AT&T Park in 2006.

3. COMERICA PARK, DETROIT

On April 11, 2000, the Detroit Tigers played their first game at Comerica Park, which was the same day as the opening of AT&T Park. No home runs were hit at the park in the first three contests but on April 14, Juan Gonzalez hit a three-run homer to cap off a four-run bottom of the third inning for the Tigers, who went on to win 10-5. This park is more pitcher-friendly than most of the others on this list, so it is no surprise that it took four games to see the first long ball. The 2005 Home Run Derby was held at Comerica and some wags dubbed it the "Warning Track Derby" before the event. However, the park turned into a hitter's paradise that night as many records were set in that Derby.

4. **MILLER PARK, MILWAUKEE**
Two new parks opened in 2001. The first was Miller Park, home of the Milwaukee Brewers. On April 6, Cincinnati Reds outfielder Michael Tucker clouted the first home run at the park—a two-run drive in the fourth inning to score the first runs at the field. Jeromy Burnitz smacked the first Brewers' homer in the sixth inning. The home team won the contest, 5-4, when Richie Sexson hit a solo shot in the bottom of the eighth inning for the winning margin. The park has a retractable fan-shaped roof that can be closed in case of bad weather.

5. **PNC PARK, PITTSBURGH**
The Pittsburgh Pirates opened their new place on April 9, 2001, three days after Miller Park in Milwaukee. The field is situated on the banks of the Allegheny River near the confluence of the Allegheny, Monongahela, and Ohio rivers. The view over the right field fence and beyond the Allegheny is the magnificent Pittsburgh skyline, beautiful day or night. Sean Casey, first baseman of the Cincinnati Reds, smacked the first homer in the top of the first inning. He was the fourth batter of the game and hit a two-run shot that gave the Reds a lead they never surrendered in the contest. Two days later the Pirates earned their first victory in the second game played in the park and right fielder John Vander Wal homered in the bottom of the third inning for the first four-bagger at the park by the Buccos.

6. **GREAT AMERICAN BALLPARK, CINCINNATI**
The Cincinnati Reds played their first contest at Great American Ballpark on March 31, 2003, and lost to the Pittsburgh Pirates, 10-1. The Pirates scored six runs in the top of the second frame, which came on the first three homers at the park. Reggie Sanders led off the scoring at the field with a

two-run homer. Four batters later, Kenny Lofton hit a three-run homer, which was followed immediately by a Jason Kendall solo shot. All three came at the expense of Jimmy Haynes, who was charged with the loss in the contest. The second game at the park was played on April 2, and right fielder Austin Kearns hit the first blast by a Red in the first inning. Ken Griffey, Jr. hit the first of his many homers at the park in the third inning that night.

7. PETCO PARK, SAN DIEGO

On April 8, 2004, the San Diego Padres opened their new home, Petco Park, with a ten-inning, 4-3 victory over the San Francisco Giants. The Giants took a 3-2 lead in the top of the 10th when Marquis Grissom led off the frame with a solo shot and the first homer at the park. This is one of the few new parks that is pitcher-friendly. Indeed, it took the Padres six games to hit their first four-bagger at Petco when Mark Loretta smacked a solo home run in the bottom of the first on April 15. Petco's most unusual feature is the 98-year-old Western Metal Supply Company building, which has been incorporated into the structure, as the left field pole is attached to the southeastern corner of the building.

8. CITIZENS BANK PARK, PHILADELPHIA

The Philadelphia Phillies played the first game in their new home on April 12, 2004, as they lost to the Cincinnati Reds, 4-1. The only run scored in the game by the home team came on a solo homer by Bobby Abreu in the bottom of the first inning. During the first season in the stadium, it was evident that the park favored home run hitters too much. After the season, the first two rows of seats in left field were removed and, starting in 2005, the wall was five feet further from home plate and two feet taller, thus cutting down on the homer-happiness of the park.

9. BUSCH STADIUM III, ST. LOUIS

On April 10, 2006, the third park to sport the name "Busch Stadium" opened to the public. Sportsman's Park was re-named Busch Stadium in 1953 and the Cardinals moved into a new stadium with that moniker in May 1966. The current park replaced that stadium. The Redbirds beat the Milwaukee Brewers in the first game at the current park, 6-4, and St. Louis went on to win the World Series that October. Bill Hall of the Brewers hit the first homer in the second inning to score the first two runs in the stadium. Cardinal favorite Albert Pujols hit a solo shot in the bottom of the third frame to inaugurate the park for the Cardinals.

10. NATIONALS PARK, WASHINGTON

The Washington Nationals inaugurated their new home on March 30, 2008, with a game against the Atlanta Braves on national television. In the top of the fourth inning, Braves third baseman Chipper Jones hit a fly ball to left-center that landed in the seats for the first home run in the new park. In the bottom of the ninth, hometown hero Ryan Zimmerman hit a pitch into the same area for a game-ending homer for the first Nationals home run in the park. It was only the third time in history that a park had opened with a game-ending four-bagger. The other two were County Stadium in Milwaukee in 1953 (Bill Bruton) and Coors Field in Denver in 1995 (Dante Bichette).

The State of Slugging

F our members of the 500 Home Run Club were born in California, the most of any state. They are Barry Bonds (born in Riverside), Mark McGwire (Pomona), Ted Williams (San Diego), and Eddie Murray (Los Angeles). Together, these four have slugged over 2,300 major league blasts. The fact that more California natives have hit 500 homers than those of any other state is no surprise, since more Californians have played major league baseball than players from any other state. A total of twelve different players from the Golden State have hit at least 375 home runs. In addition to the hitters with 500, Darrell Evans (Pasadena), Duke Snider (Los Angeles), Jason Giambi (West Covina), Graig Nettles (San Diego), Dwight Evans (Santa Monica), Jim Edmonds (Fullerton), Matt Williams (Bishop), and Jeff Kent (Bellflower) have all proven their slugging ability. Here are the other states with multiple players who have hit at least 375 homers.

1. MARYLAND
Five players from Maryland have reached 375 career homers. Two of those hit more than 500: Babe Ruth (Baltimore) and Jimmie Foxx (Sudlersville). Cal Ripken (Havre de Grace) hit over 400, while both Al Kaline (Baltimore) and Harold Baines (Easton) slugged 375 or more. Ruth and Foxx were

the first two players to hit 500 home runs and they are both Maryland natives. Since there was no major league team in Maryland at that time, neither Ruth nor Foxx homered in their native state but the other three hitters each slugged many home runs in the Old Line State.

2. **ALABAMA**

Alabama natives Hank Aaron (Mobile), Willie Mays (Westfield), and Willie McCovey (Mobile) all slugged 500 four-baggers. In addition, Billy Williams (Whistler) hit 426 dingers in his career. Mays in 1969 and Aaron in 1971 were the second and third players in history to hit at least 600 home runs. None of these sluggers ever hit a big league four-bagger in Alabama because there has never been a major league game played in the Yellowhammer State.

3. **TEXAS**

Three members of the 500 Home Run Club were born in Texas: Frank Robinson (Beaumont), Ernie Banks (Dallas), and Eddie Mathews (Texarkana). Norm Cash (Justiceburg) hit 377, most of them for the Tigers. All four players hit home runs in the Lone Star State during their careers.

4. **PENNSYLVANIA**

Ken Griffey, Jr. (Donora) and Reggie Jackson (Wyncote) both mashed 500 homers. Stan Musial (Donora) hit 475 and Mike Piazza (Norristown) also topped the 400 milestone. Of the four players, only Jackson never hit a home run in the Keystone State, as he spent his entire career in the American League.

5. **OKLAHOMA**

Three of the top sluggers from Oklahoma spent their entire careers with one team. Mickey Mantle (Spavinaw) hit 536 home runs with the Yankees, Willie Stargell (Earlsboro) slugged 475 homers for the Pirates, and Johnny Bench (Oklahoma City) hit 389 with the Reds. Joe Carter (Oklahoma City) clouted 396 playing for multiple teams. No major league games have ever been played in the Sooner State.

6. FLORIDA

Florida has no native sons with 500 homers but four with at least 375 dingers. Fred McGriff and Gary Sheffield (both Tampa) are each well over 450 career homers. Andre Dawson (Miami) hit 438, including his last ten with the Florida Marlins. Chipper Jones (Deland) joined this group in 2007. All four sluggers homered in the Sunshine State.

7. NEW YORK

In 2007, Alex Rodriguez (New York City) became the first native of the state to join the 500 Home Run Club. Lou Gehrig (New York City) hit 493 homers and Carl Yastrzemski (Southhampton) hit 452. Since both ARod and Gehrig played for the Yankees, they hit many homers in the Empire State. Yastrzemski hit 21 at Yankee Stadium as a visitor.

8. OHIO

Mike Schmidt (Dayton) hit 548 homers for the Phillies and Frank Howard (Columbus) slugged 382 four-baggers in his career while playing for multiple teams in both leagues. Both Schmidt and Howard slugged home runs in the Buckeye State during their careers.

9. LOUISIANA

Mel Ott (Gretna) was the third slugger to hit 500 career home runs. Albert Belle (Shreveport) saw his career cut short due to an arthritic hip after hitting 381 homers. After the 1998 season, Belle was the single-season leader in homers for two different teams, the Indians (50) and the White Sox (49). Jim Thome beat his record with Cleveland in 2002. No major league games have been played in the Pelican State.

10. OREGON

Dave Kingman (Pendleton) hit homers for four different teams in 1977—one in each division that existed that season. Dale Murphy (Portland) won back-to-back National League Most Valuable Player Awards in 1982 and 1983. Kingman slugged 442 and Murphy 398 major league homers, but none were hit in the Beaver State since no major league games have ever been played there.

Hey, Pops!

Most baseball players finish their careers before turning 40 years old. However, many continue to play effectively well into their forties. The guys who became the oldest to homer at each defensive position and at designated hitter are documented here. By the way, the oldest pinch hitter to hit a four-bagger is Julio Franco, who did so for the New York Mets on April 20, 2006, at the age of 47 years 240 days, and turned a 2-1 deficit into a 3-2 advantage against the San Diego Padres in an eventual Mets victory.

1. PITCHER

On June 27, 1930, Jack Quinn of the Philadelphia (now Oakland) Athletics hit the last homer of his career while pitching a victory over the St. Louis Browns (now Baltimore Orioles). The dinger came in the second game of that day's doubleheader. No other pitcher is within three years of Quinn's age when homering that day: 46 years 361 days. He was just four days away from his 47th birthday!

2. CATCHER

Hall of Famer Carlton Fisk hit 351 home runs as a catcher in his career, which was the record when he retired. The last came on April 7, 1993, while playing for the Chicago White Sox. Fisk holds nine of the top ten spots on the list of oldest catchers to homer. Only Merv Shea in 1944 gets on the list in the number five slot. Fisk's oldest came at the age of 45 years 102 days.

3. FIRST BASEMAN

Julio Franco, the oldest pinch hitter to homer, is also the oldest first baseman to hit a four-bagger. In fact, Franco is the name in all ten top spots at this position. The last came on May 4, 2007, while playing for the New York Mets. Franco was 48 years and 254 days old when he smacked this homer. Franco is the only player in history to hit a four-bagger after his 47th birthday and he actually hit two after turning 48!

4. SECOND BASEMAN

Jimmy Dykes hit 108 major league home runs. The last came on August 24, 1938, while Dykes played second base for the Chicago White Sox. This circuit clout was hit at Yankee Stadium when Dykes was 41 years 287 days old. Craig Biggio, who retired in 2007, has eight of the top ten spots on the second baseman list, including second place at 41 years 250 days.

5. THIRD BASEMAN

Graig Nettles hit two homers as a third baseman on June 27 and 28, 1987—the last two he hit at third base. For the latter dinger, Nettles was 42 years 312 days old. The top ten spots on the list for oldest by a third baseman are held by Nettles and Darrell Evans, with six of them hit by Nettles. This was not the last homer of Nettles career, as he hit two more as a pinch hitter in 1987 and 1988.

Julio Franco, the oldest player to hit a home run in
major league history. *Atlanta Braves*

6. SHORTSTOP

Luke Appling hit the last home run of his career on August
26, 1949, while playing shortstop for the Chicago White Sox.
Appling was 42 years 146 days old when he stroked that
four-bagger and holds five of the top six spots on the shortstop list. Appling once hit a homer in an exhibition game at
RFK Stadium when he was 75 years old.

7. LEFT FIELD

Rickey Henderson homered on July 20, 2003, at the age of 44 years 207 days. This, the last homer of Henderson's career, came as the first batter of the game for the Los Angeles Dodgers, the 81st lead off homer of his career, which is still the record for that category. Henderson holds the top six spots on the left field "old guy" list.

8. CENTER FIELD

This name should sound familiar: Rickey Henderson. In addition to left field, Henderson hit the oldest homer as a center fielder on April 27, 2002. Rickey, 43 years and 123 days old that day, hit the homer as the first batter of the game for the Boston Red Sox. He is the only 43-year-old to hit a homer as a center fielder.

9. RIGHT FIELD

Sam Rice, playing right field for the Cleveland Indians, hit a home run on June 15, 1934, at the age of 44 years 115 days. Enos Slaughter holds seven of the top nine spots on the right field list, with Rice also at number six.

10. DESIGNATED HITTER

Designated hitter is a position that many older sluggers take in the lineup in order for a team to make use of their bat without putting the player in the field defensively. Julio Franco is the oldest player to hit a homer, so it should be no surprise that he is the oldest designated hitter to homer. He hit one on June 14, 2005, at the age of 46 years 295 days to top this list. Thus, Franco is the oldest at three spots: designated hitter, pinch hitter and first base. Carl Yastrzemski holds nine places on the top ten list for old designated hitters.

Birthday Buddies

There are many cases of two major league players being born on the exact same day. Usually, this is not a fact that is given much attention but sometimes it can provide a humorous note. The following batters homered more than once in their careers off a pitcher who shared the same birthday—month, day and year.

1. PODGE WEIHE
John Garibaldi "Podge" Weihe was born on November 13, 1862, in Cincinnati. He played 64 major league games in 1883 and 1884, hitting four homers in the latter season for the Indianapolis Blues of the American Association. Two of those home runs came in the same game on September 20, at home against the Richmond Virginias—both off pitcher Pete Meegan. Meegan was born on November 13, 1862, in San Francisco and played in 42 total major league games. However, among the eight home runs he surrendered, he gave up two to a batter born on the same day. That they performed this feat is amazing given the small number of games played by each of them.

2. BOBBY THOMSON

Bobby Thomson was born in Glasgow, Scotland, on October 25, 1923, and Russ Meyer was born on the same day in Peru, Illinois. On July 5, 1950, Thomson, playing center field for the New York Giants, homered off Meyer in Philadelphia. Thomson repeated the feat twice: once on July 11, 1953, with Meyer now pitching for the Brooklyn Dodgers and once on May 30, 1956. By 1956, Thomson was playing for the Milwaukee Braves and Meyer for the Chicago Cubs.

3. WILLIE DAVIS

Willie Davis, who played 18 years in the majors, was born on April 15, 1940, in Mineral Springs, Arkansas. He hit 182 home runs in his career and twice in 1968 homered off Woodie Fryman, a pitcher with the Phillies. Fryman was born on April 15, 1940, in Ewing, Kentucky. The homers came on April 17 in Philadelphia and August 10 in Los Angeles.

4. REGGIE SMITH

On May 28, 1974, St. Louis Cardinals outfielder Reggie Smith hit a three-run home run off Dodger hurler Don Sutton in St. Louis. Smith was born in Shreveport, Louisiana on April 2, 1945, and Sutton on the same day in Clio, Alabama. Eight years later, Smith, now with the San Francisco Giants, hit a solo homer off Sutton, who was now pitching for the Houston Astros. This is the longest span between homers of any pair on this list.

5. TOM BRUNANSKY

Tom Brunansky, born August 20, 1960, in Covina, California, played 14 years in the majors and hit 271 home runs. Six of those home runs came off Mark Langston, who was born August 20, 1960, in San Diego, about 120 miles from Covina.

The unusual part of this pairing is that they faced each other in both the American and National Leagues, with Bruno homering five times in the AL and once in the NL off Langston. The six are the most homers of any pair on this list.

6. ANDY VAN SLYKE
Andy Van Slyke played 13 years in the majors and has been known as a guy always ready with a quip. Roger McDowell pitched 12 years in the majors and was known as a practical joker. It was inevitable, then, that these two guys, both born on December 21, 1960, would pair up for a couple of home runs. On June 7, 1987, Van Slyke, who was born in Utica, New York, homered twice off McDowell, who was born in Cincinnati. The Pirates center fielder hit a home run to lead off the tenth inning of the first game of a doubleheader and then hit his second off McDowell in the eighth inning of game two. The Pirates and Mets split the doubleheader.

7. EDGAR MARTINEZ
Edgar Martinez hit 309 home runs in his 18-year career with the Seattle Mariners. Martinez, born in New York City on January 2, 1963, was a seven-time All Star in his career. On June 17, 1994, he homered in Kansas City off Royals pitcher David Cone, who was born in Kansas City on January 2, 1963. The next season, on August 24, Martinez slugged another four-bagger off Cone, who was now pitching for the New York Yankees. This home run was hit in Seattle's Kingdome.

8. LARRY WALKER
Larry Walker was born on December 1, 1966, in Maple Ridge, British Columbia, Canada. The same day in Knoxville, Tennessee, future big league pitcher Greg McMichael was born. Twenty-nine years later Walker, playing for the Colorado

Rockies, hit a home run off McMichael in Atlanta on May 18, 1995. Two years later, Walker homered off McMichael again, this time on May 16, 1997. McMichael was now pitching for the Mets and the homer came at Shea Stadium.

9. MANNY RAMIREZ

Slugger Manny Ramirez and pitcher Scott Eyre were both born on May 30, 1972, Ramirez in Santo Domingo, Dominican Republic and Eyre in Inglewood, California. On July 18, 1998, Ramirez, playing right field for the Cleveland Indians, homered in Chicago off Eyre, who was pitching for the White Sox. Ramirez got Eyre again on April 17, 2002, after both players had changed teams. Ramirez was now a member of the Boston Red Sox and Eyre was pitching for the Toronto Blue Jays. The blast was hit in Toronto.

10. TONY CLARK

Tony Clark was born in Newton, Kansas on June 15, 1972. Playing for the Detroit Tigers, he homered off Yankees pitcher Ramiro Mendoza on April 18, 1999. Medoza was born on the same day as Clark in Los Santos, Panama. On June 30, 1999, Clark again homered off a Yankee pitcher, Andy Pettitte. Pettitte was also born on June 15, 1972, in Baton Rouge, Louisiana. Thus, Clark hit two home runs off two different pitchers born on the same day as he was born—certainly, a very unique feat.

Standing Short and Going Long

Sluggers are generally thought to be big guys, tall and muscular. However, there have been quite a few batters shorter than 5'9" who could pound the ball out of the yard at rates that match the "big boys." Here are the top guys in that category, and there are no Napoleon complexes here! By the way, the shortest player in history was Eddie Gaedel, who pinch-hit as a stunt in 1951 and is listed at 3'7"—he walked in his one plate appearance and never appeared in a game again.

1. YOGI BERRA
Lawrence Berra grew up in St. Louis and was given his nickname by a boyhood friend. Berra, a 14-time All Star, won three American League Most Valuable Player Awards in his career with the Yankees. At 5'7-1/2", Berra is among the shortest players ever but slugged 358 home runs in his Hall of Fame career.

2. JOE MORGAN
Joe Morgan played most of his career for the Houston Astros and Cincinnati Reds, hitting 268 home runs. When he retired, Morgan had hit more home runs as a second baseman (266)

than any other player in history. The 5'7" Morgan won back-to-back Most Valuable Player Awards in the National League, played in nine All Star Games, and was elected to the Hall of Fame in 1990.

3. HACK WILSON
The shortest player on this list, Hack Wilson, stood 5'6" tall. Wilson led the National League in homers four times, including three consecutive years. He held the NL single-season record (56) for home runs from 1930 until it was broken in 1998, and hit 244 four-baggers in his career. This Hall of Famer had his best years with the Chicago Cubs.

4. KIRBY PUCKETT
Minnesota Twins outfielder Kirby Puckett may be best known for a home run he hit in the 1991 World Series. However, the 5'8" Puckett smacked 207 during his 12-year career, which was shortened by glaucoma. The ten-time All Star was named the Most Valuable Player in the 1993 Midsummer Classic and was elected to the Hall of Fame in 2001.

5. RAY DURHAM
Ray Durham has played primarily for the Chicago White Sox and San Francisco Giants in his career. The 5'8" second baseman has hit 192 homers through 2008, including 34 as the first batter of the game for his team.

6. TIM RAINES, SR.
Two members of the Raines family have played in the major leagues, both named Tim. The dad, a 5'8" outfielder, hit 170 four-baggers in his career, most of which was spent with the Montreal Expos and Chicago White Sox. Father and son played together for a few games with the Baltimore Orioles at the

end of the 2001 season. His son never homered in his brief major league career.

7. SMOKY BURGESS
Smoky Burgess hit 126 home runs in his career. The 5'8-1/2" player was the catcher in Harvey Haddix's "perfect" game and played for the 1960 Pittsburgh Pirates, who won the World Series when Bill Mazeroski hit a series-ending home run. Burgess hit 16 pinch-hit home runs out of his 145 total pinch hits.

8. JIMMY ROLLINS
Oakland native Jimmy Rollins made his debut with the Phillies in late 2000 and has played for that team since then. Through 2008, the 5'8" shortstop has hit 125 four-baggers. He was the 2007 NL Most Valuable Player and has played in three All-Star Games.

9. CHET LAABS
Chet Laabs played 11 years from 1937 through 1947 in the American League and this 5'8" outfielder hit 117 home runs during that time. He played with the St. Louis Browns in the 1944 World Series and represented the Browns in the 1943 All Star Game.

10. PAUL WANER
Paul Waner and his brother, Lloyd, are both in the Hall of Fame. Paul, at 5'8-1/2", was the shorter of the two. He hit 113 home runs in his long career spent mostly with the Pittsburgh Pirates. His brother was too tall to qualify for this list.

Large Strike Zones Don't Stop These Guys

These sluggers tower over their teammates and most of the rest of the world. Taller, stronger players are the prototypical home run hitters and this group, all at least 6'5", hit a lot of long balls in their collective careers. The tallest player in history is pitcher Jon Rauch at 6'11", who has not hit a home run but has surrendered a few in his career.

1. MARK MCGWIRE

Mark McGwire set the single-season record for homers in 1998 when he slugged 70 four-baggers. This was one of four times the 6'5" McGwire hit 50 in a season. In his career, he hit 583 home runs for the Oakland Athletics and St. Louis Cardinals.

2. FRANK THOMAS

There have been two guys named Frank Thomas who played in the majors. The second one stands 6'5" and joined the 500 Home Run Club on June 28, 2007. He has hit 521 homers though the 2008 season, playing most of his career with the Chicago White Sox.

3. **DAVE WINFIELD**
Dave Winfield, at 6'6", was a star college basketball player and then was drafted by the Atlanta Hawks in the NBA. The 12-time All Star hit 465 career home runs playing for six teams, mostly the San Diego Padres and New York Yankees. He was elected to the Hall of Fame in 2001.

4. **DAVE KINGMAN**
Dave Kingman played for seven teams in 16 seasons, including four in 1977. The 6'6" Kingman hit 442 homers in his career, including one in each of the four existing divisions during that 1977 season. No other player ever performed that feat.

5. **FRANK HOWARD**
Frank "Hondo" Howard, the tallest player on this list, hit 382 homers in his career. The 6'7" outfielder was named the 1960 National League Rookie of the Year while with the Los Angeles Dodgers and played in four All Star Games. While playing for the Washington Senators, Howard was called "The Capitol Punisher," a nickname that was appropriate given his many tape-measure homers into the upper deck at RFK Stadium.

6. **DAVE PARKER**
Dave Parker, the 1978 National League Most Valuable Player, hit 339 home runs in his career. The 6'5" Parker was named the 1979 All Star MVP for throwing out two base runners in that game. He played most of his career with the Pittsburgh Pirates and Cincinnati Reds.

7. **DARRYL STRAWBERRY**
Darryl Strawberry was named the 1983 National League Rookie of the Year. Early in his career, he hit many long home

runs and led the NL in that category in 1988. However, drug and legal problems limited his playing time and the 6'6" out-fielder ended his career with 335 home runs.

8. **RICHIE SEXSON**

Richie Sexson has hit 306 home runs through 2008. The 6'6" first baseman has played for a number of teams in his career and hit 45 homers in two different seasons for the Milwaukee Brewers.

9. **TROY GLAUS**

Third baseman Troy Glaus, the 2002 World Series Most Valu-able Player while playing for the Anaheim Angels, stands 6'5". Through the 2008 season, Glaus has hit 304 homers. He smacked three in the 2002 World Series.

10. **ADAM DUNN**

Adam Dunn, who debuted in 2001, has spent most of his career with the Cincinnati Reds. Through 2008, the 6'6" Dunn has slugged 278, including four consecutive season with at least 40. He is the career leader in four-baggers at Great American Ballpark in Cincinnati, with 124 through 2008.

Instant Karma

A community that gains a major league sports franchise is energized by the civic pride that comes from the fact that other people now think of them as a "big league city." This self-esteem turns into instant karma, as tourism usually increases in the community, thus bringing more money into the area. This chapter talks about the last ten expansion teams and the batter who slugged the first home run for each of them. The first round of expansion took place in the early 1960s, as the two leagues, each of which had had eight teams since 1901, added two teams. Here are the ten teams added after 1962.

1. KANSAS CITY ROYALS, 1969

The Royals played their first American League game on April 8, 1969, beating the Minnesota Twins, 4-3, in 12 innings. Their first home run was not hit until their fifth game on April 13, when first baseman Mike Fiore led off the second inning in Oakland with a four-bagger. This started the Royals on the way to a 4-1 victory over the Athletics.

2. **SEATTLE PILOTS, 1969**

The Seattle Pilots also started play in the American League in 1969. Their first game, played on April 8, featured a home run by right fielder Mike Hegan, the second batter in the history of the club. The Pilots won the contest, 4-3, in Anaheim against the Angels. The following season, the team moved to Milwaukee and became the Brewers. Danny Walton hit the first two homers for the Wisconsin edition of the club on April 11, 1970.

3. **MONTREAL EXPOS, 1969**

The National League also added two teams in 1969. The Montreal Expos, the first club to play outside the United States, won their first game on April 8, by beating the New York Mets in New York, 11-10. In that contest, the Expos hit three home runs, the first a solo shot in the fourth inning by pitcher Dan McGinn. In 2005, the Expos moved to Washington, D.C., becoming the Nationals. On April 4, outfielder Terrmel Sledge (what a great name for a slugger—"Sledge hammers the ball into the seats!") hit the first four-bagger for the Nationals.

4. **SAN DIEGO PADRES, 1969**

The other National League team that started play in 1969 was the San Diego Padres. They played their initial game on April 8 hosting and beating the Houston Astros, 2-1. The first Padres run scored on a home run by third baseman Ed Spiezio in the fifth inning that tied the score at 1-1. Spiezio's home run was the first hit in Padres history.

5. **SEATTLE MARINERS, 1977**

The next expansion took place eight years later as the American League added two teams, to create two seven-team divisions. The Seattle Mariners, added to the AL West, played their first game on April 6, losing to the Angels, 7-0. Juan Bernhardt hit the first home run for the club on April 10, in the fifth game of the season. The clout came in the fifth inning of a 12-5 loss to the Angels.

6. TORONTO BLUE JAYS, 1977
The Toronto Blue Jays, added to the American League East, played their initial contest on April 7, 1977, in Toronto. The 9-5 victory over the Chicago White Sox was powered by three circuit clouts. First baseman Doug Ault, the third batter in the history of the club, hit the first homer to gather the first hit and score the first run in franchise history. Ault homered again in the third frame and then, in the fifth, Al Woods made his major league debut by pinch-hitting and smashing a home run on the first pitch he saw in the big leagues.

7. COLORADO ROCKIES, 1993
Sixteen years after the American League expanded, the National League followed suit by adding two teams in 1993. The Colorado Rockies, based in Denver, became the first major league team in the Mountain Time Zone. They played their first game on April 5, losing in New York to the Mets, 3-0. Two days later, right fielder Dante Bichette scored the first run in franchise history by hitting the team's first home run in the seventh inning of a 6-1 loss to the Mets.

8. FLORIDA MARLINS, 1993
The Florida Marlins, based in Miami/Dade County, played their first game on April 5, 1993, as they beat the Los Angeles Dodgers, 6-3. On April 12, catcher Benito Santiago homered in the seventh game in club history. The clout came in the sixth inning of a 4-3 loss to the Giants in 11 innings in San Francisco.

9. ARIZONA DIAMONDBACKS, 1998

In 1998, two teams were added to the majors, one in each
league. However, in order to keep an even number of clubs
in each circuit, the Milwaukee Brewers moved from the AL to
the NL as part of the expansion. The Arizona Diamondbacks
played their first game on March 31, 1998, losing at home to
the Colorado Rockies, 9-2. Both Diamondback runs were
scored on solo home runs and the first was by first baseman
Travis Lee in the sixth inning.

10. TAMPA BAY DEVIL RAYS, 1998

The new American League club in 1998 was the Tampa Bay
Devil Rays. They lost their first game on March 31 to the Detroit Tigers, 11-6. Third baseman Wade Boggs smacked the
first home run in Devil Rays history in the sixth inning, driving
in the first two runs in club history.

Wild Thing, You Move Me

S ince 1904, only 11 teams have moved from one city to another. Usually, that move is accompanied by a lot of negative publicity in the losing location and positive publicity in the gaining location. The Boston Braves moved to Milwaukee after the 1952 season to start this caravan of franchises. The last home run hit by a Boston Braves player came in Brooklyn on September 27, 1952, when third baseman Eddie Mathews hit three blasts to drive the Braves to an 11-3 victory. The last Braves homer in Boston had come on September 19, as catcher Walker Cooper hit a two-run dinger in the fourth inning. Here is a list of sayonara home runs for each club before they loaded the moving vans.

1. ST. LOUIS BROWNS TO BALTIMORE

After the 1953 season, the Browns moved to Baltimore to become the Orioles. This was the second time the franchise changed locations, as they started in Milwaukee in 1901, before leaving for the "Show Me State" the next season. The Browns lost all three games in the final series in St. Louis and, on September 26, shortstop Billy Hunter hit a two-run home run in the eighth inning to cap the Browns home run history.

2. PHILADELPHIA ATHLETICS TO KANSAS CITY

For the third consecutive year, a team changed cities. This time it was the Athletics leaving Philadelphia for Kansas City, which supplanted St. Louis as the western-most city in the majors. The last homer for the Philadelphia version of the squad was hit by first baseman Lou Limmer, who hit a solo homer at Yankee Stadium on September 25, 1954. Don Bollweg hit the final home run in Philadelphia by the home team on September 18.

3. BROOKLYN DODGERS TO LOS ANGELES

Two teams moved from greater New York City to California after the 1957 season. The Brooklyn Dodgers left Ebbets Field, moving to Los Angeles for the 1958 season. On September 28, 1957, third baseman Randy Jackson hit the last Brooklyn homer in a game played in Philadelphia. The last Dodger home runs in Brooklyn were on September 22, as center fielder Duke Snider hit two off Robin Roberts, in the fifth and seventh innings.

4. NEW YORK GIANTS TO SAN FRANCISCO

The New York Giants left the Polo Grounds after the 1957 season and moved to San Francisco. The last two homers by the New York edition of the club were hit by first baseman Gail Harris on September 21 in Pittsburgh. The last Giants home run hit in New York came on September 8, when Hank Sauer hit one against their cross-town rivals, the Brooklyn Dodgers.

5. WASHINGTON SENATORS TO MINNEAPOLIS

Three of the moves on this list involve Washington, D.C. The first exodus from the nation's capital occurred when the Washington Senators, a charter club in the American League, moved to Minneapolis after the 1960 season to become the Minnesota Twins. The last Senator to homer was right fielder Bob Allison on September 28, 1960. He hit the four-bagger against the New York Yankees at Washington's Griffith Stadium three days from the end of the season.

6. MILWAUKEE BRAVES TO ATLANTA

The team that started all the shifting in 1952 moved again after the 1965 season. The Milwaukee Braves became the Atlanta Braves, where they remain in the 21st century. Gene Oliver hit the last circuit drive for the Milwaukee club on October 2, the penultimate day of the season. It provided the only run of the day for the Braves off Sandy Koufax, who beat them, 3-1, in Los Angeles. The last Braves four-bagger in Milwaukee was hit in the last home game on September 22 by the same Gene Oliver, an inside-the-park home run and the last of three hit that day by the Braves, as they beat the Dodgers in 11 innings, 7-6.

7. KANSAS CITY ATHLETICS TO OAKLAND

The Athletics, who had moved to Kansas City for the 1955 season, moved much further west after the 1967 campaign. On the last day of the season, October 1, catcher Dave Duncan hit the last home run by the Missouri version of the squad at Yankee Stadium off Mel Stottlemyre. Ramon Webster had hit the last four-bagger in Kansas City on September 2 against the Baltimore Orioles.

8. SEATTLE PILOTS TO MILWAUKEE

The expansion Pilots played one year in Seattle and moved to Milwaukee only a week before the start of the 1970 season. Pilots left fielder Steve Whitaker hit a solo homer in the ninth inning on October 2, 1969, for the only run of their last game, as they lost to the Oakland Athletics, 3-1. Just as 1969 was the only year for the Pilots, it was the only season that Sick's Stadium was used by a major league team. Whitaker hit the last of 167 home runs at the park.

9. WASHINGTON SENATORS TO TEXAS

When the Senators moved to Minnesota in 1961, an expansion team, confusingly called the Washington Senators, was created to replace them in the District of Columbia. This edition of the Nats played from 1961 through 1971 before moving to Arlington, Texas, becoming the Texas Rangers. The last game played by the Senators on September 30, 1971, at RFK Stadium in D.C. was forfeited to the New York Yankees with two out in the top of the ninth inning and the home team ahead, 7-5. Frank "Capital Punisher" Howard provided one of the seven runs with a home run in the sixth inning. Since the Senators were ahead when the game was forfeited, the "official" score of the game is 9-0 in favor of the Yankees. Thus Howard homered in a game in which his team officially scored no runs!

10. MONTREAL EXPOS TO WASHINGTON

After 33 years of stability in the major leagues, the most recent team to relocate moved after the 2004 season. The Expos, who had played in Montreal since 1969, ended their existence on October 3 at Shea Stadium in New York, which was the same location as their first game 35 years before. On October 2, Brad Wilkerson hit a three-run homer in the ninth inning to provide the winning advantage in the Expos last win, 6-3. On September 28, Juan Rivera knocked in the only runs in a 5-2 loss to the Florida Marlins for the last homer hit in Montreal by an Expo player.

Broadcaster Calls Describing Memorable Home Run Moments

There have been many home runs that have come at critical, high-tension moments and decided important games. Those events have often been described with élan and the recordings of these calls get replayed frequently because of the high-visibility of the event. Here are some of the best.

1. "IN THE YEAR OF THE IMPLAUSIBLE, THE IMPOSSIBLE HAS HAPPENED."

On October 15, 1988, in game one of the World Series, the Oakland Athletics led, 4-3, with two out and a runner on first base in the bottom of the ninth inning. The Athletics had their Hall of Fame closer, Dennis Eckersley pitching. Kirk Gibson, the Dodgers' team leader, limped to the plate on two bad legs to pinch hit. Gibson did not start the game because of his ailments and was unlikely to play the next day. On a 3-2 count, Gibson hit a line drive into the right field seats with nothing more than an upper-body and arm swing to win the game, 5-4, in very dramatic fashion. As he limped around the bases, Gibson continually pumped his arms in celebration of the victory, one of the most memorable World Series moments of all time and Gibson's only appearance in the Series that year. Vin Scully described the event on network television in his usual intelligent, literate manner. Scully has broadcast games for the Dodgers starting in 1950 in Brooklyn and moving with the club to Los Angeles in 1958. He won the Ford C. Frick Award in 1982.

2. "I DON'T BELIEVE WHAT I JUST SAW!"

Jack Buck called the Gibson World Series game on network radio and voiced the thoughts of many of the viewers as Gibson rounded the bases. Buck, the long-time voice of the

Long-time Dodger broadcaster Vin Scully. *Los Angeles Dodgers*

St. Louis Cardinals, won the Ford C. Frick Award in 1987. When he joined the Cardinals broadcast team in 1954, he was paired with Harry Carey, and remained with the Cardinals until his death in 2002. He and former player Mike Shannon worked together starting in 1972, making their pairing one of the longest running in baseball broadcasting history.

3. "THE GIANTS WIN THE PENNANT, THE GIANTS WIN THE PENNANT, THE GIANTS WIN THE PENNANT, THE GIANTS WIN THE PENNANT!"

Bobby Thomson hit what is arguably the most heard home run of all time on October 3, 1951, in the last of a three-game playoff to determine the National League champion. The Brooklyn Dodgers were ahead, 4-2, with one out in the bottom of the ninth inning at the Polo Grounds. Thomson's three-run, game-ending, pennant-clinching homer into the left field seats was captured on film and is one of the most replayed dingers in baseball history, partly because of its importance in New York history, and partly because it is one of the earliest recordings of its type. Russ Hodges, the Giants' broadcaster, went crazy as he kept yelling into his microphone.

4. "LAST HALF OF THE NINTH. THE GIANTS CHANCES LOOK GRIM, ALMOST NIL . . . HERE IT IS. BRANCA PUMPS, DELIVERS. A DEEP DRIVE TO LEFT FIELD. IT IS A HOME RUN! AND THE NEW YORK GIANTS WIN THE NATIONAL LEAGUE PENNANT AND THE NEW YORK CROWD GOES WILD."

On the other side of that 1951 game, Red Barber of the Dodgers saw his team defeated and the season end on an improbable last-minute homer. Barber broadcast games for the

Cincinnati Reds (1934–38), the Brooklyn Dodgers (1939–53), and the New York Yankees (1954–66). Barber was colorful and innovative in his broadcasts and known for phrases such as referring to his perch in the "Catbird Seat" while watching games. Barber won the Ford C. Frick Award in 1978.

5. "THE 1-0 DELIVERY TO FISK. HE SWINGS . . . LONG DRIVE, LEFT FIELD . . . IF IT STAYS FAIR, IT'S GONE . . . HOME RUN! THE RED SOX WIN! AND THE SERIES IS TIED, THREE GAMES APIECE!"

Game 6 of the 1975 World Series between the Boston Red Sox and Cincinnati Reds, played on October 21 at Fenway Park, has been called the best World Series game ever played by many writers. It ended when Carlton Fisk hit a home run off the left field pole in the bottom of the twelfth inning, one of the most memorable four-baggers in history because of the game situation and the physical gyrations performed by Fisk as the ball sailed down the line. Long-time Boston broadcaster Ned Martin described the homer for New England fans on Red Sox radio.

6. "GO CRAZY, FOLKS, GO CRAZY! . . . A HOME RUN BY THE WIZARD! . . . GO CRAZY!"

Ozzie Smith, the light-hitting shortstop of the St. Louis Cardinals, hit one of the most improbable game-ending home runs of all time on October 14, 1985, in game five of the National League Championship Series. The switch-hitting Smith hit the ball batting left-handed for the first lefty homer of his eight-year career—in fact, he had only hit 13 total home runs to that point in his career. Jack Buck called the game on the Cardinals radio network.

7. **"IT'LL BE AN 0-2 PITCH. AND HE HITS IT TO DEEP LEFT! HEEP GOES BACK. IT IS GONE! HOLY COW! OH, MY GOODNESS! I DON'T BELIEVE IT! I DON'T BELIEVE IT! RICK CAMP! RICK CAMP! I DON'T BELIEVE IT! THAT CERTIFIES THIS GAME AS THE WACKIEST, WILDEST, MOST INCREDIBLE GAME IN HISTORY!"**

The New York Mets played a 19-inning game in Atlanta on July 4, 1985. Pitcher Rick Camp surrendered an unearned run in the top of the 18th frame because of his own throwing error. In the bottom of the inning, Camp had to bat because the Braves used all 15 non-pitchers in the game by that point. With two out and seemingly no chances left for the Braves, Camp hit the only homer of his nine-year major league career over the left field wall. The Mets won the game in the 19th inning with five runs scored off Camp. Fate laughed as Camp again batted in the 19th with two outs. This time, however, Camp struck out to end the contest. The Braves shot off the planned fireworks show even though it was 3:55am when the game finished due to multiple rain delays and the extra innings. Braves announcer John Sterling made the call on Camp's four-bagger.

8. **"SWING AND A DRIVE . . . DOWN THE LEFT FIELD LINE . . . THIS ONE'S GOT A CHANCE . . . CURLING . . . GONE! . . . IT'S GONE! . . . ALEX GONZALEZ AND THE MARLINS HAVE DONE IT!"**

The Florida Marlins beat the New York Yankees in six games in the 2003 World Series. In game four, played on October 22, the Marlins tied the series at two games each with a dramatic twelfth-inning homer from light-hitting shortstop Alex Gonzalez. The ball dropped over the fence in the left field corner between the scoreboard and the pole. Jon "Boog"

Sciambi, who acquired the nickname because of his resemblance to former Orioles star John "Boog" Powell, made this call on Marlins radio.

9. "HE'S SITTING ON 714. HERE'S THE PITCH BY DOWNING . . . THERE'S A DRIVE INTO LEFT-CENTER FIELD! THAT BALL IS GONNA BEEEEEEE . . . OUTTA HERE! IT'S GONE! IT'S 715! THERE'S A NEW HOME RUN CHAMPION OF ALL TIME! AND IT'S HENRY AARON!"

One of the most recognized home run calls of all time was by then Braves broadcaster Milo Hamilton on April 8, 1974, as Hank Aaron passed the most-famous number in all of sports. This call has been played thousands of times since 1974, especially as Barry Bonds approached Aaron's record in 2007.

10. "THREE AND TWO TO BONDS . . . EVERYBODY STANDING HERE AT 24 WILLIE MAYS PLAZA . . . AN ARMADA OF NAUTICAL CRAFT GATHERED IN MCCOVEY COVE BEYOND THE RIGHT FIELD WALL . . . BONDS ONE HOME RUN AWAY FROM HISTORY . . . AND HE SWINGS, AND THERE'S A LONG ONE DEEP INTO RIGHT-CENTER FIELD, WAY BACK THERE, IT'S GONE! A HOME RUN! INTO THE CENTER FIELD BLEACHERS TO THE LEFT OF THE 421 FOOT MARKER. AN EXTRAORDINARY SHOT TO THE DEEPEST PART OF THE YARD. AND BARRY BONDS WITH 756 HOME RUNS HAS HIT MORE HOME RUNS THAN ANYONE ELSE WHO HAS EVER PLAYED THE GAME!"

Jon Miller called this one on the San Francisco Giants radio network on August 7, 2007, as Bonds passed Hank Aaron on the career leader board. Miller had missed many of Bonds' milestones due to his work with ESPN but called this one for the home fans.

Hey, Buddy,
I'm a Hall of Famer!

T he Hall of Fame has many members who were outstand
ing pitchers. One of them, Cy Young, even has a pitching
award named after him. However, even the best players have
less-than-perfect moments and, although most pitchers are
not great hitters, they occasionally do hit the ball out of the
park. The following American League Hall of Fame pitchers
hit a home run off another Hall of Fame pitcher. This is unlikely to happen again because of the designated hitter rule.
Pitchers in the American League now only hit in interleague
games.

1. CY YOUNG OFF ADDIE JOSS
On June 5, 1902, Cy Young, pitching for the Boston Americans (now Red Sox), hit an inside-the-park homer off Addie
Joss of the Cleveland Broncos (now Indians). The clout came
in the third inning and scored the first run of the eventual 3-2
Boston victory. Young scored the winning run in the eighth
inning.

2. EDDIE PLANK OFF CY YOUNG
Eddie Plank, pitching for the Philadelphia (now Oakland) Athletics, hit an inside-the-park home run on May 2, 1903, in

Boston off Cy Young. The solo homer plated the third and last run in the Athletics 3-0 victory.

3. JACK CHESBRO OFF CY YOUNG

Mr. Young figures into the action again on April 14, 1904, when Jack Chesbro, hurler for the New York Highlanders (now Yankees), hit a ball to the deepest part of center field for an inside-the-park blow in the second inning on Opening Day in New York. The Highlanders scored five runs in the first and never looked back in the 8-2 victory. So Cy Young was involved in the first three times this feat was accomplished in the American League.

4. WALTER JOHNSON OFF ED WALSH

Walter Johnson hit 23 home runs in his career, good for ninth place all-time on the list of homers by pitchers. On June 6, 1912, "The Big Train" came into the game in relief with the bases full of White Sox runners in the sixth inning and preserved the game for the Washington Senators (now the Minnesota Twins). Johnson then hit a two-run homer into the left field seats in the seventh frame off Ed Walsh to put the game out of reach, as the Senators won, 9-1.

5. WALTER JOHNSON OFF HERB PENNOCK

Nearly a year later, on May 26, 1913, Johnson again clouted a home run off a fellow Hall of Famer. This time the victim was Herb Pennock of the Philadelphia (now Oakland) Athletics and the blow came in the fourth inning of the second game played in Philadelphia that day. Johnson pitched seven innings in the 9-2 victory.

6. RED FABER OFF HERB PENNOCK

Herb Pennock shows up twice on this list surrendering a home run. On June 6, 1923, ten years after the home run by Walter

Johnson, Red Faber of the Chicago White Sox hit the first homer of his career as the Chicago South Siders defeated Pennock and the New York Yankees, 4-1, in New York. The four-bagger came in the seventh inning and provided the winning advantage.

7. TED LYONS OFF WAITE HOYT
White Sox hurler Ted Lyons hit two home runs off two different Hall of Famers. The first came on September 26, 1930, off Waite Hoyt of the Detroit Tigers in the fifth inning in Detroit. The visiting Sox beat the Tigers, 3-1 at Navin Field, later called Tiger Stadium.

8. TED LYONS OFF RED RUFFING
Four years later, Lyons hit his second home run off a Hall of Fame pitcher, this time victimizing Red Ruffing of the Yankees. The homer was part of a huge uprising against the first place Yankees, as the last place Pale Hose won, 14-2 in Chicago on May 23, 1934.

9. RED RUFFING OFF HAL NEWHOUSER
Six years after being taken deep by Ted Lyons, Red Ruffing hit a three-run homer off Hal Newhouser of the Tigers on July 30, 1940. The Yankees won the contest played in Detroit, 8-6. Ruffing clouted 34 home runs in his career, fourth on the all-time list for pitchers.

10. BOB LEMON OFF EARLY WYNN
The last time an American League Hall of Fame pitcher homered off another Hall of Famer took place on July 29, 1946, when Bob Lemon of the Cleveland Indians smacked the four-bagger off Early Wynn of the Washington Senators.

The solo blast was hit in the seventh inning of the second game of the doubleheader that day as the Senators beat the Indians in Cleveland, 8-4. Lemon hit 35 home runs in his career, the second most of any pitcher in history.

The Spelling Checker in My Computer Didn't Like This List

In the 2005 movie *Derailed*, a question is asked about the seven players with 11-letter last names who each hit 40 or more home runs in a season. This is a bad question, since the parameters do not produce an answer—there are not seven such players. However, this is proof that many people are fascinated by long and short names. For example, a guy who hit 511 home runs, Mel Ott, has one of the shortest names of any player in history. But it is the longer names that can be difficult to spell for writers and difficult to proofread for editors. (I must remember to tell my editor that these names are spelled correctly, even though some of them look like a line on an eye chart.) Here are the guys with at least ten letters in their last names who hit 30 or more home runs in a single season.

1. CARL YASTRZEMSKI

Carl Yastrzemski played 23 years for the Boston Red Sox and hit 452 home runs in his career. Yaz topped the 40-homer milestone in three seasons by hitting 44 in 1967 and 40 in 1969 and 1970. His next highest total was 28 in 1977, so he never had a season total between 30 and 39—very strange! There are 11 letters in Yastrzemski's last name—tied for the most on this list.

2. NOMAR GARCIAPARRA

Nomar Garciaparra started his career in Boston, playing for the Red Sox from 1996 through July 2004. In 1997, Nomar hit 30 homers and followed the next season with 35. He has not hit 30 in one season since, playing for the Chicago Cubs and Los Angeles Dodgers. There are 11 letters in Garciaparra's last name, and his first name is "Ramon" spelled backwards.

3. TED KLUSZEWSKI

Ted Kluszewski played for the Reds, Pirates, White Sox, and Angels in his 15-year career. Big Klu smashed at least 30 home runs each season from 1953 through 1956, topping out at 49 in 1954, when he led the National League. There are ten letters in Kluszewski.

4. ROY CAMPANELLA

Roy Campanella played for the Brooklyn Dodgers from 1948 through 1957. Campy hit at least 30 homers four times, with 31 in 1950, 33 in 1951, 41 in 1953, and 32 in 1955. There are ten letters in his last name.

5. DARRYL STRAWBERRY

Darryl Strawberry, the 1983 National League Rookie of the Year, started his career with the Mets, where he hit over 30 homers in 1987 (39), 1988 (39), and 1990 (37). His production and time on the field dropped after that, as he had many personal problems. There are ten letters in his last name.

6. TONY CONIGLIARO

Tony Conigliaro played for the Red Sox from 1964 until he was beaned on August 18, 1967, hitting 32 home runs in 1965. He was the American League Comeback Player of the Year in 1969 and hit 36 homers the next season but had more eye problems after that and played few games in 1971 for the Angels and 1975 for the Red Sox. There are ten letters in his last name.

7. **RICO PETROCELLI**
Rico Petrocelli played one game for the 1963 Red Sox and then from 1965 through 1976 for the club. He slugged 40 home runs in 1969 for the BoSox but never hit more than 29 in any other season. There are ten letters in Petrocelli.

8. **PETE INCAVIGLIA**
Pete Incaviglia played for six teams from 1986 through 1998. He hit 30 home runs as a rookie with the Texas Rangers in 1986, but never matched that production again, as he slugged 27 his sophomore year, and never more than 24 after that. There are ten letters in Incaviglia.

9. **MIKE PAGLIARULO**
Mike Pagliarulo played for five teams from 1984 through 1993 and in 1995. He hit 32 homers in 1987 for the Yankees after hitting 28 the previous year. Pagliarulo never hit more than 19 in any other season. There are ten letters in Pagliarulo.

10. **MIKE LIEBERTHAL**
Mike Lieberthal started his career in 1994 and played for the Phillies through the 2006 season. He hit 31 home runs in 1999, but never more than 20 for the club in any other season. In 2007, he played for the Los Angeles Dodgers, but did not slug any home runs that season. There are ten letters in Lieberthal.

Double Your Pleasure, Double Your Fun

Slugging 50 home runs in one season is considered a great feat as only 25 players have hit at least 50 homers in one year. The following guys have performed that feat more than once, which truly is a Ruthian accomplishment. This is in order by most seasons slugging 50 circuit clouts.

1. BABE RUTH, 4
Babe Ruth hit at least 50 homers in one season four times in his career. He was the first to hit 50 in any season and thus the first slugger to hit 50 in multiple seasons. In 1920, Ruth swatted 54, followed it with 59 in 1921, and then hit 60 in 1927. In each of these years he set a new single-season record. In 1928 Ruth hit 54 and in 1930 he barely missed when he slugged 49. The Babe swatted at least 40 homers for seven consecutive seasons (1926-32), which is still the record. All of these homers were hit for the Yankees.

2. MARK MCGWIRE, 4
Mark McGwire hit at least 50 homers in four consecutive years from 1996 through 1999. He whacked 52 for the Athletics in 1996, and hit 58 the next year, with 34 for the Athletics and

24 for the Cardinals. In 1998, Big Mac set a new single-season record by hitting 70 homers and followed that with 65 in 1999. He played for the Cardinals the latter two seasons.

3. SAMMY SOSA, 4
Sammy Sosa repeated the feat first performed by Mark McGwire when he hit at least 50 homers in four consecutive seasons. In 1998, Sosa smashed 66 for the Cubs and followed with 63, 50, and 64. He led the league in 2000, but finished second each time he hit over 60.

4. ALEX RODRIGUEZ, 3
Alex Rodriguez hit 50 in consecutive seasons with the Texas Rangers. In 2001, he smacked 52 and followed with 57 the next season. In 2007, he topped the 50 milestone for the third time when he slugged 54 for the New York Yankees. He led the American League all three seasons.

5. JIMMIE FOXX, 2
Jimmie Foxx was the second player in history to have multiple seasons of 50-plus homers. In fact, he was only the third player to hit 50 in a season, after Babe Ruth and Hack Wilson. Foxx slugged 58 in 1932 for the Philadelphia (now Oakland) Athletics and then 50 in 1938 for the Red Sox. Only Foxx, McGwire and ARod have hit 50 homers in a season for two different clubs.

6. RALPH KINER, 2
Ralph Kiner was the first National League player to hit at least 50 homers twice. In 1947, Kiner hit 51 for the Pirates and he slugged 54 in 1949 for the Bucs. Kiner smacked 40-plus homers for five consecutive years starting in 1947.

7. **MICKEY MANTLE, 2**
Mickey Mantle played his entire career with the Yankees and twice hit 50 homers for the squad, becoming the second Bronx Bomber to accomplish the feat (after Ruth). The Mick hit 52 in 1956 and 54 in 1961.

8. **WILLIE MAYS, 2**
Willie Mays hit 51 homers in 1955 for the New York Giants at the age of 24. Mays then hit 52 in 1965 for the San Francisco Giants. He is the only player to hit 50 twice for the same team in different cities.

q. **KEN GRIFFEY, JR., 2**
Ken Griffey, Jr. hit exactly 56 home runs in consecutive seasons, doing so in 1997 and 1998 for the Seattle Mariners. He led the major leagues the first year and the American League the second time.

10. **CECIL AND PRINCE FIELDER, 1 + 1**
Okay, so this is really a father and son duo rather than one player. Cecil Fielder hit 51 home runs for the Detroit Tigers in 1990 after playing in Japan the previous season. His son, Prince, hit 50 in 2007 for the Milwaukee Brewers and thus the Fielders became the first family members to each slug 50 in a season. Prince is the youngest player to hit 50 in a season, reaching the milestone as a 23-year-old.

You Hit It Where?

There are 28 cities that are home to a major league baseball team, with two teams in New York and two in Chicago. There are many cities that have had a major league team in the past but are no longer part of the big leagues. The following group of cities has never been home for a team but has had major league games played and home runs hit there.

1. SAN JUAN, PUERTO RICO

On April 1, 2001, the Toronto Blue Jays opened the Major League season by hosting the Texas Rangers at Estadio Hiram Bithorn in San Juan, Puerto Rico. Shannon Stewart of the Jays hit the first big league homer in the park named for the first native of Puerto Rico to play in the major leagues. In 2003 and 2004, the Montreal Expos played 43 games in San Juan as their alternate home park. There were a total of 101 homers hit in the 44 major league games, with Brian Schneider of the Expos hitting six to top the individual list.

2. TOKYO, JAPAN

On March 29–30, 2000, the Chicago Cubs and New York Mets opened their season in Tokyo with two games at Tokyo

Dome. Then on March 30–31, 2004, the New York Yankees and Tampa Bay Devil Rays played a two-game series in the Dome and in March 2008, the Red Sox and Athletics played two games. Shane Andrews hit the first major league homer in Japan on March 29, 2000. Jorge Posada of the Yankees hit two at the Dome, the only player to hit more than one in Tokyo. Sixteen home runs were hit in the six games, including the first career homer for Brandon Moss of the Red Sox in 2008.

3. HONOLULU, HAWAII
The San Diego Padres hosted the St. Louis Cardinals for three games on April 19 and 20, 1997, playing a doubleheader on the first day. Ron Gant of the Cardinals hit the only major league home run in the Aloha State on April 20 when he hit the ball into the left-center field gap. Gant circled the bases for an inside-the-park home run before the fielders could retrieve the baseball.

4. MONTERREY, MEXICO
The San Diego Padres hosted the New York Mets for three games from August 16 through 18, 1996, at Estadio de Beisbol Monterrey. Steve Finley hit the first major league homer in Mexico as the eighth batter in the first game. The Padres later hosted the Colorado Rockies in Monterrey on April 4, 1999. Ten home runs were hit in the four games played in Monterrey with Ken Caminiti of the Padres hitting three of them.

5. LAS VEGAS, NEVADA
At the beginning of the 1996 season, the Oakland Athletics played their first home stand at Cashman Field, Las Vegas, due to incomplete football renovations at their own park in

Oakland. Domingo Cedeno of the Blue Jays hit the first major league four-bagger in Nevada on April 1. Scott Brosius and Bobby Higginson each hit three that week and 23 home runs were hit at the park in six games.

6. JERSEY CITY, NEW JERSEY
In 1956 and 1957, the Brooklyn Dodgers played 15 games at Roosevelt Stadium in Jersey City. The original plan was that each opponent would play one game there each season but the Phillies played two in 1957. Wally Moon of the Cardinals stroked the first homer at the stadium on May 16, 1956, and 13 were hit in the 15 games. Duke Snider of the Dodgers and Eddie Mathews of the Braves each hit two in New Jersey during the two-year experiment.

7. LAKE BUENA VISTA, FLORIDA
The Tampa Bay Devil Rays played a three-game series against the Texas Rangers in May 2007, at The Ballpark at Disney's Wide World of Sports in Lake Buena Vista, Florida, the spring training home of the Atlanta Braves. Eight homers were hit there with Hank Blalock of the Rangers hitting the first. Victor Diaz and Delmon Young each smacked two homers at the park. The Rays hosted the Toronto Blue Jays for three days in April 2008, and five more round-trippers were slugged in that series. Matt Stairs hit two in one game.

8. CANTON, OHIO
On September 18, 1890, the Pittsburgh Alleghenys (now Pirates) hosted the Cleveland Spiders at Mahaffey Park in Canton, Ohio. Four home runs were hit that day, with Bill Delaney of the Spiders whacking the first of them. The Cleveland Broncos (now Indians) played three Sunday games at the park in 1902 and 1903 and three more homers were struck in the

American League games. No batter hit more than one home run in Canton, now the home of the Pro Football Hall of Fame.

9. WHEELING, WEST VIRGINIA

The Pittsburgh Alleghenys (now Pirates) hosted the New York (now San Francisco) Giants at Island Grounds in Wheeling, West Virginia on September 22, 1890. Jesse Burkett of the Giants hit the only homer that day in the ninth inning.

10. DAYTON, OHIO

On Sunday, June 8, 1902, the Cleveland Broncos (now Indians) hosted the Baltimore Orioles (now New York Yankees) at Fairview Park, Dayton, Ohio. Roger Bresnahan of the Orioles hit the only circuit drive of the game, a three-run inside-the-park homer in the eighth inning.

Ten Guys
with Hobbies

Often, a person will start a sentence with something along the lines of "Back when I was a boy . . ." and then proceed to tell some tall tale. Well, many years ago there were a lot of two-sport athletes playing Major League Baseball and in the National Football League. Here are ten guys who hit at least one home run in the big leagues and played in the NFL. Special mention should be made of George Halas, who played briefly for the 1919 New York Yankees, and Greasy Neale, who played eight years in the big leagues for the Reds and Phillies. Halas did not hit a home run but was one of the founders of the National Football League. Neale was a Hall of Fame NFL coach in the 1940s. (Thanks to Bob Davids for the chapter title.)

1. TOM BROWN

There have been a number of ballplayers named Tom Brown. This one is Thomas William Brown, who played for the 1963 Washington Senators and hit one homer on September 9 at DC (now RFK) Stadium. He joined the Green Bay Packers as a defensive back for the 1964 season and played there through 1968, playing in the first two Super Bowls. In 1968, Brown scored two touchdowns, one on a punt return and one on a fumble recovery. In 1969, he played one game for the Washington Redskins. In his career, Brown played 71 NFL games with 13 interceptions.

2. BO JACKSON

Heisman Trophy winner Bo Jackson played for the Kansas City Royals from 1986 through 1990, the Chicago White Sox in 1991 and 1993, and the California Angels in 1994, hitting 141 home runs in that time. He also homered in the 1989 All Star Game and was named the Most Valuable Player in that contest. He was a running back for the Los Angeles Raiders from 1987 through 1990, playing both sports simultaneously. During a Raiders playoff game in January 1991, he was injured and underwent hip-replacement surgery in early 1992. When he returned to baseball in 1993 with the new hip, his first at bat was a pinch-hit home run. As a part-time player for the Raiders, he scored 18 touchdowns and he starred in a series of television commercials for Nike featuring the slogan "Bo Knows."

3. CARROLL HARDY

Carroll Hardy played for the Indians, Red Sox, and Colt .45s (now the Astros) from 1958 through 1964, and the Twins in 1967, hitting 17 home runs in his big league career. He had already played for the 1955 San Francisco 49ers as a half back. In ten games, he scored four touchdowns on pass receptions.

4. DEION SANDERS

"Neon Deion" Sanders played part time for the Yankees, Braves, Reds and Giants from 1989 through 1995, and the Reds again in 1997 and 2001. He homered 39 times with five of those in the American League. In the NFL, he played for the Atlanta Falcons, San Francisco 49ers, Dallas Cowboys, and Washington Redskins from 1989 through 2000, and the Baltimore Ravens in 2004-05. Sanders primarily played corner back and had one sack, 53 interceptions and ten touchdowns. On the offensive side of the line, he scored 12 touchdowns as a receiver and kick returner. He earned two Super Bowl rings and played in the 1992 World Series. He homered and scored a touchdown within five days in September 1989.

5. CHARLIE BERRY
Charlie Berry played for the Philadelphia Athletics, Boston Red Sox and Chicago White Sox most years from 1925 through 1938. He hit 23 home runs in his career as a catcher. From 1942 through 1962, he umpired in the American League, working 3,080 games as an arbiter. In 1925–26, Berry played for the Pottsville Maroons in the NFL. He scored 92 points in his career, including nine touchdowns, three field goals and 29 points after touchdowns.

6. JIM THORPE
Olympic Gold Medalist Jim Thorpe played for the New York Giants, Cincinnati Reds, and Boston Braves from 1913 through 1919 and hit seven home runs. He played in the NFL in the 1920s, including for the New York Giants. He was a running back, pass receiver, and also threw passes in his career. In the early 1920s, he also coached the teams on which he played.

7. BRIAN JORDAN
Brian Jordan played for the Cardinals, Braves, Dodgers, and Rangers from 1992 through 2006 and smashed 184 home

runs as an outfielder. He played as a defensive back and kick return specialist for the Atlanta Falcons from 1989 through 1991. Although he never scored a touchdown in the NFL, he did score four points via two safeties. In 2005, while playing right field for the Braves at RFK Stadium, he dove for a fly ball and seemed to have it in his glove, only to have it pop out when he struck the ground. The scoring on the play was a hit for the batter, the official scorer commenting that the ground cannot cause a fumble.

8. VIC JANOWICZ

Vic Janowicz played in the major leagues and in the NFL at the same time. He was a member of the Pittsburgh Pirates squad in 1953–54, hitting two home runs. In 1954–55, he was a halfback for the Washington Redskins, scoring seven touchdowns, kicking 10 field goals and 37 extra points.

9. GARLAND BUCKEYE

Garland Buckeye pitched for the Washington Senators in 1918, and the Cleveland Indians and New York Giants from 1925 through 1928. He hit five homers in the American League with the Indians in 1925–26. In between stints in the major leagues, Buckeye was a lineman for the Chicago Cardinals football club from 1920 through 1924. He is credited with one pass interception in 1924.

10. WALT FRENCH

Walt French played outfield for the Philadelphia Athletics in 1923 and 1925–29, hitting two home runs in his career. Meanwhile, he was a running back for the Pottsville Maroons in 1925, scoring five touchdowns.

All in the Family

There are many examples of multiple people from the same family playing in the major leagues. When the relations are brothers, they are usually playing concurrently and many times on the same team. Here are some examples of families with at least three people who have homered in the big leagues. These relationships are grandfather/father/son and brothers only, even though there are many examples of cousins, uncles and nephews and other more distant relationships.

1. THE ALOU FAMILY

Three Alou brothers played in the major leagues in the 1960s. Felipe played from 1958 through 1974, hitting 206 home runs, Matty from 1960 through 1974, hitting 31 home runs, and Jesus from 1963 through 1979 with 32 homers. The three brothers played in the outfield together three times in 1963 for the Giants. Moises, son of Felipe, made his debut in 1990 and has hit 332 homers through 2008. Moises has homered for teams managed by his dad, and against teams managed by his dad. All four Alous have played in the World Series.

2. THE BOONE FAMILY

Ray Boone played in the majors from 1948 through 1960 and hit 151 home runs. His son, Bob, played in the majors from 1972 through 1990, hitting 105 homers. Bob has two sons who have played in the big leagues. Bret played from 1992 through 2005 and smacked 252 four-baggers, while Aaron made his debut in 1997 and has hit 120 homers through 2007. All four Boones have played in the All Star Game and World Series.

3. THE BELL FAMILY

David Russell "Gus" Bell played in the National League from 1950 through 1964, hitting 206 home runs. His son, David Gus "Buddy" Bell, played from 1972 through 1989 and hit 201 home runs. Buddy has two sons who have played major league baseball. David Michael Bell, the third member of the Bell family named David, but the first to be called David, played from 1995 through 2006, hitting 123 homers. His younger brother, Mike, played 19 games in 2000 and hit two round-trippers.

4. THE SCHOFIELD FAMILY

John Richard "Ducky" Schofield played from 1953 through 1971 and hit 21 homers. His son, Dick, played from 1983 through 1996, hitting 56 homers. Both were known as good-fielding shortstops. Ducky's daughter, Kim, had a son named Jayson Werth, who made his debut in 2002 and has hit 57 home runs through 2008. Jayson is the son of a former minor league player and the stepson of big leaguer Dennis Werth, who hit three home runs in a four-year career.

5. THE COONEY FAMILY

James Joseph "Jimmy" Cooney hit all four of his major league homers in 1890 for the Chicago Colts (now Cubs) in the first year of a brief big league career. His son, James Edward "Jimmy" Cooney, hit the first of his two major league home runs in 1924 while playing for the St. Louis Cardinals. They were the first father/son pair to each hit a major league home run. The younger son, Johnny, also played in the majors and hit both his career homers on consecutive days in 1939 for the Boston Bees.

6. THE DIMAGGIO FAMILY

Hall of Famer Joe DiMaggio played for the Yankees from 1936 through 1951 and hit 361 home runs. His older brother, Vince, played in the National League from 1937 through 1946 and hit 125 homers. Dom DiMaggio, the youngest of the trio, played for the Red Sox from 1940 through 1953 and hit 87 homers. Both Joe and Dom lost playing time to World War II. All three California natives played in the All Star Game.

7. THE ALLEN FAMILY

Dick Allen hit 351 home runs in his big league career that ran from 1963 through 1977. His older brother, Hank, played from 1966 through 1973 and hit six homers. They were teammates on the White Sox in 1972–73. Younger brother Ron played seven games in 1972 and hit one home run.

8. THE ALOMAR FAMILY

Sandy Alomar hit 13 home runs in his big league career playing for six teams from 1964 through 1978. His son, Sandy, made his big league debut in 1988 and hit 112 homers. Younger son Roberto played from 1988 through 2004 and hit 210 homers. All three played in the All Star Game.

q. **THE NIEKRO FAMILY**

Hall of Famer Phil Niekro pitched in the majors from 1964 through 1987 and hit seven home runs. Younger brother Joe pitched in the big leagues from 1967 through 1988 and hit his one major league home run off his brother on May 29, 1976. Joe's son, Lance, made his debut in 2003 and has hit 17 home runs.

10. **THE CRUZ FAMILY**

Jose Cruz hit 165 major league home runs while playing from 1970 through 1988. His younger brother, Hector, played from 1973 through 1982 and hit 39 circuit clouts. Brother Tommy played seven games in the mid-1970s but did not homer. Jose's son, Jose, made his debut in 1997 and hit 204 home runs.

Hey, I'm a "Star" in the Series

Many players have been selected for the All Star Game and played in the World Series in the same year. Far fewer of them have hit home runs in one or the other event but the toughest task is to hit a four-bagger in both the All Star Game and the World Series in the same season. Sixteen players have accomplished this feat. Here are the ten American league sluggers to do it.

1. LOU GEHRIG

Lou Gehrig, known as the "Iron Horse" for his streak of playing 2,130 consecutive games from 1925 through 1939, hit a home run in the 1936 All Star Game at Braves Field in Boston. This was Gehrig's first four-bagger in the star extravaganza, which had started in 1933. In consecutive games in the 1936 Fall Classic on October 3 and 4, Gehrig homered against the New York Giants, both at Yankee Stadium. The following season, Larrumpin' Lou repeated his feat of the previous season by homering in the All Star contest at Griffith Stadium, Washington, and in the fourth game of the 1937 World Series at the Polo Grounds. Gehrig hit two circuit drives in All Star competition and ten in the World Series.

2. **JOE DIMAGGIO**

Joltin' Joe DiMaggio, like his teammate Lou Gehrig, played his entire career with the New York Yankees. His only All Star homer was hit in the 1939 game played at Yankee Stadium. In the 1939 World Series, the Yankees played the Cincinnati Reds and DiMaggio hit one of his eight career World Series homers. The blast came at Crosley Field in Cincinnati in the third game of the four game sweep by the Bronx Bombers.

3. **MICKEY MANTLE**

Mickey Mantle was the third player to homer in both events in the same season. Mantle played his entire career with the Yankees and is the all-time leader for homers in the Fall Classic, with 18 in 12 Series appearances. Mantle homered in both the All Star Game and the World Series in consecutive years, 1955–56. The 1955 Star classic was played at County Stadium, Milwaukee and Mantle capped off the four-run first inning with a three-run shot off Robin Roberts. Mantle played in three games of the 1955 Fall Classic and homered in the second inning of the third game, played at Ebbets Field in Brooklyn. In 1956, Mantle homered in the All Star Game played at Griffith Stadium in Washington and three times in the World Series against the Brooklyn Dodgers.

4. **HARMON KILLEBREW**

Harmon Killebrew played most of his career with the team now known as the Minnesota Twins. He made his debut in 1954 when the team was still the Washington Senators and continued with the franchise through the 1974 season. (He played one final year with the Kansas City Royals in 1975.) In 1965, the All Star Game was played Metropolitan Stadium in Bloomington, Minnesota, Killebrew's home park. He homered in the fifth inning of that game as his American League squad lost, 6-5. That fall, the Twins lost to the Los Angeles Dodgers in the World Series in seven games and Killebrew hit his only home run in the Fall Classic in game four in Los Angeles.

5. FRANK ROBINSON

Hall of Famer Frank Robinson has a long resume of awards and honors. He played in 11 All Star Games, hitting two home runs—one in each league. In 1971, playing for the Baltimore Orioles and the American League, Robinson hit a four-bagger at Tiger Stadium, Detroit. That fall, the Birds played in the World Series against the Pittsburgh Pirates and Robinson smacked two homers in the seven-game series. The first was at home in Memorial Stadium in game one and the other was at Three Rivers Stadium in Pittsburgh in game three.

6. SANDY ALOMAR, JR.

Sandy is one of three Alomars to play in the All Star Game, as his father, Sandy, and his brother, Roberto, have also appeared in the Midsummer Classic. Sandy, Jr. homered in the 1997 game at Jacobs Field in Cleveland and in October played in the World Series with the Indians. Alomar clouted two homers in the Series, one at Pro Player Stadium (now Dolphins Stadium) and one at the Jake (now Progressive Field).

7. DEREK JETER

Through the 2008 season, Derek Jeter has played in nine All Star Games and six World Series. In 2001, the Yankee captain homered at Safeco Field in Seattle in the sixth inning of the Midsummer Classic and then in game four of that year's World Series at Yankee Stadium. The 2001 Series started a week late since the season was delayed a week by the tragic events on September 11. Jeter's game-ending home run, officially on October 31, was after midnight, so in real time it was the first major league home run ever hit in November. However, the official date is still October 31 for that home run.

8. JASON GIAMBI

Jason Giambi signed with the New York Yankees for the 2002 season after spending the first seven years of his career with the Oakland Athletics. In 2003, Giambi played in his fourth All Star Game and hit his first home run in the Midsummer Classic. That fall, Giambi played in his first World Series, as the Yankees lost to the Florida Marlins in six games. Giambi homered in game five in Florida off closer Braden Looper when the game was lost for the Yankees.

9. DAVID ORTIZ

The Boston Red Sox won the World Series in 2004, partly due to the home runs of two sluggers, David Ortiz and Manny Ramirez. Ortiz, who joined the Sox for the 2003 season, played in his first All Star Game in 2004 and homered in the sixth inning at Minute Maid Park in Houston. That fall, Ortiz had two game ending home runs in the post-season, one in the Division Series and one in the League Championship Series. He is the only batter to perform that feat through 2008. In his first World Series at bat on October 23, 2004, Ortiz homered over the Fenway Park bullpens in right field.

10. MANNY RAMIREZ

Two Red Sox teammates performed this feat in 2004. Manny Ramirez, playing in his sixth All Star Game, hit his first home run in the Midsummer Classic when he connected off Roger Clemens in the first inning in Houston. In October, Ramirez homered in the first inning of game three of the World Series, as the Red Sox swept the Cardinals to win for the first time since 1918. Ramirez had played in the Series twice with the Cleveland Indians, in 1995 and 1997.

David Ortiz circles the bases after hitting a home run to end the 2004 American League Division Series. *Julie Cordeiro/Boston Red Sox*

new York State of Mind

Through the years, many batters have played a great ma jority of their games in one state. Therefore, some sluggers have had the opportunity to hit many home runs in one state. California has five teams, with three of them in the National League West, thus allowing players in that division to play most of their games in a season in California and consequently many chances to hit a four-bagger in the Golden State. New York City had three teams for many years and two of them were in the National League, thus providing the same opportunity in the Empire State at that time. Here is a list of the most home runs hit by one batter in one state.

1. BARRY BONDS, CALIFORNIA

Barry Bonds left the Pittsburgh Pirates and signed with the San Francisco Giants for the 1993 season, having already played many games in California while with the Pirates. After changing teams, Bonds played his home games in California and had two league opponents there as well: the Los Angeles Dodgers and the San Diego Padres. Bonds smacked 383 four-baggers in California, with 300 in San Francisco, 43 in San

Diego and 29 in Los Angeles. He also hit 11 in Interleague games in California, with eight in Oakland and three in Anaheim.

2. MEL OTT, NEW YORK
Mel Ott played for the New York Giants from 1926 through 1947 and hit 323 homers at the Polo Grounds, the most by any player in one park. Ott also whacked 25 at Ebbet's Field in Brooklyn for a total of 348 in the state of New York.

3. BABE RUTH, NEW YORK
Babe Ruth called two parks home while he played for the New York Yankees: the Polo Grounds from 1920 through 1922 and Yankee Stadium, "The House that Ruth Built," from 1923 through 1934. He swatted 85 homers at the Polo Grounds, including ten as a visitor with the Red Sox. Ruth then hit 259 four-baggers at Yankee Stadium for a total of 344 in the Empire State.

4. SAMMY SOSA, ILLINOIS
Sammy Sosa played most of his career with the Chicago Cubs, although he also played over two years with the White Sox. He hit 293 home runs in the friendly confines of Wrigley Field, 11 at Comiskey Park (now closed) and eight more at the new Comiskey Park (now called U.S. Cellular Field). Thus, Sosa has hit a total of 312 in Illinois.

5. WILLIE MCCOVEY, CALIFORNIA
Willie "Stretch" McCovey started his career in 1959 with the San Francisco Giants, for whom he played until 1973. He also played for the San Diego Padres and Oakland Athletics before finishing his career with the Giants. McCovey hit 521 big league homers, 298 of which he smacked in California.

This includes 32 in San Diego, 22 in Los Angeles, and 244 in San Francisco. He hit eight at Seals Stadium and 236 at Candlestick Park in San Francisco, 5 at LA Memorial Coliseum and 17 at Dodger Stadium.

6. ERNIE BANKS, ILLINOIS

Ernie Banks played his entire career with the Chicago Cubs. He hit 290 of his 512 home runs at Wrigley Field but never played at any other park in Illinois. His 290 in the Prairie State qualifies for sixth all-time on this list and second in the state behind Sammy Sosa.

7. MIKE SCHMIDT, PENNSYLVANIA

Mike Schmidt is the only slugger to qualify for this list in a state other than California, New York or Illinois, as he played his entire career with the Philadelphia Phillies and many road games in Pittsburgh. Schmidt hit 265 of his 548 homers at Veterans' Stadium in Philadelphia and 25 at Three Rivers Stadium in Pittsburgh. Thus, his total in the Keystone State is 290 home runs.

8. FRANK THOMAS, ILLINOIS

Frank Thomas started his career with the White Sox in 1990 and played for that club through 2005. Through the 2008 season, Thomas has hit 267 home runs in the Windy City, with two at Wrigley Field, two at Comiskey Park (now closed), and 263 at U.S. Cellular Field. He is third in Illinois home runs behind Sammy Sosa and Ernie Banks, but at the top of the Illinois list for American Leaguers.

9. MICKEY MANTLE, NEW YORK

Mickey Mantle hit more home runs at Yankee Stadium than any other player in history, as his 266 outpace Babe Ruth's

259 at the stadium in the Bronx. This is Mantle's entire New York output, as he did not play regular season games in any other venue in the Empire State.

10. **WILLIE MAYS, CALIFORNIA**

When the New York Giants moved to San Francisco for the 1958 season, center fielder Willie Mays moved with them and slugged 264 circuit drives in the state of California. Willie hit 235 homers in San Francisco, with 32 at Seals Stadium and 203 at Candlestick Park. He also clouted 12 at LA Memorial Coliseum and 11 at Dodger Stadium. Toward the end of his career, he played as a visitor in San Diego and hit six in that city, including his 600th clout in 1969.

Me and My Shadow

For a team to have two great sluggers is a boon to the offense since more power usually equates to more runs and, consequently, more wins for the team. If two hitters play together for many years, there is more opportunity for both to homer in the same game. Here is the list of top pairs of sluggers who have homered in the same game as teammates the most times.

1. HANK AARON AND EDDIE MATHEWS, BRAVES

Hank Aaron and Eddie Mathews played together for the Braves from 1954 in Milwaukee through 1966 in Atlanta. In that time, Aaron hit 442 four-baggers and Mathews 421. In those 13 years, the pair each hit at least one home run in the same game 75 times. Aaron and Mathews are both members of the 500 Home Run Club, as Aaron stroked 755 career homers and Mathews hit 512.

2. LOU GEHRIG AND BABE RUTH, YANKEES

When Lou Gehrig played his first game with the Yankees in 1923, Babe Ruth was the star of the team and remained so until he left the Yankees after the 1934 campaign. In those seasons, Ruth swatted 496 home runs and Gehrig 348. They paired up to hit home runs in the same game 73 times, which was the record until Aaron and Mathews broke it. Ruth paired with another teammate, Bob Meusel, to swat four-baggers in the same contest 47 times. Ruth swatted 714 and Gehrig 493 career homers, the top two career totals when Gehrig retired in April 1939.

3. WILLIE MAYS AND WILLIE MCCOVEY, GIANTS
A pair of Willies, Mays and McCovey, played together for the San Francisco Giants from McCovey's debut in July 1959, until Mays was traded to the New York Mets in May 1972. During that time, they combined to hit home runs in the same game 68 times. Both are members of the 500 Home Run Club—Mays with 660 and McCovey with 521.

4. GIL HODGES AND DUKE SNIDER, DODGERS
Gil Hodges and Duke Snider played for the Brooklyn and Los Angeles Dodgers as teammates from 1947 through 1961, and then with the New York Mets in the first few weeks of the 1963 season. They hit home runs in the same game 67 times as teammates with the Dodgers, but never with the Mets in the short time they were teammates in Flushing. Snider hit 407 homers in his career and Hodges 370.

5. RON SANTO AND BILLY WILLIAMS, CUBS
Ron Santo made his debut with the Chicago Cubs in 1960 and joined teammate Billy Williams on the squad through the 1973 season. The two players combined to homer in the same game 64 different times in those 14 seasons. Santo hit 342 homers in his career, 337 of them with the Cubs. Williams smacked 426 home runs in his career, with 392 of them for Chicago. For most of the time they were teammates, there

was another slugger on the club, Ernie Banks, who hit 512 home runs. Banks and Santo homered in the same game 43 times, while Banks and Williams did so 42 times. Although the pairings with Banks do not make the top ten in this category, they were quite a trio.

6. BOB ALLISON AND HARMON KILLEBREW, SENATORS/TWINS

Bob Allison and Harmon Killebrew played together for the Washington Senators from late 1958 through the 1960 season and moved with the club to Minnesota for the 1961 season, where the team is called the Twins. They continued as teammates until Allison retired after the 1970 season and hit home runs in the same game 61 times as teammates for the franchise.

7. ANDRUW AND CHIPPER JONES, BRAVES

Chipper Jones debuted with the Atlanta Braves in late 1993 and then started playing regularly in 1995. Andruw Jones came to the big leagues with the Braves in August 1996 and was Chipper's teammate through the 2007 season. In that time, they homered in the same game 59 times.

8. (TIE) JOE ADCOCK AND EDDIE MATHEWS, BRAVES

Joe Adcock joined the Milwaukee Braves in 1953 after three years in Cincinnati and played for them through the 1962 season. Adcock, who slugged 336 career homers, and Eddie Mathews hit homers in the same game 56 times. Adcock and Hank Aaron homered in the same game 37 times.

9. (TIE) DWIGHT EVANS AND JIM RICE, RED SOX

Dwight Evans played for the Boston Red Sox from late 1972 through 1990 and finished his career with one season in Baltimore. Jim Rice joined the Red Sox in late 1974 and played in Boston his entire career, which lasted until 1989. In their years together, the two players hit homers in the same game 56 times for the BoSox, tied with Adcock and Mathews on the all-time list. Evans finished with 385 and Rice with 382 career four-baggers.

10. YOGI BERRA AND MICKEY MANTLE, YANKEES

Yogi Berra made his debut with the New York Yankees near the end of the 1946 season and played for them through 1963. Mickey Mantle played for the Yankees from 1951 through 1968. In their 13 years as teammates, Berra and Mantle homered in the same game 55 times. Berra hit 358 homers in his career and Mantle hit 536.

Things to Know to Win a Bar Bet

Many people like to amaze their friends and even complete strangers with little-known facts. Often, friendly conversations tend toward these kinds of trivial nuggets and sometimes the talk progresses to the point of one person trying to top the other with their knowledge of the game. Here are some home run facts that will amaze your friends and hopefully stump your rivals.

1. AMERICAN LEAGUE SINGLE-SEASON LEADER
Since 1998, a few sluggers have hit more than 60 home runs, including Barry Bonds and his record-setting 73 in 2001. However, all those guys played in the National League. The single-season home run record in the American League is the 61 hit by Roger Maris in 1961.

2. BABE RUTH'S FIRST HOME RUN VICTIM
Babe Ruth hit 714 home runs and single-handedly changed baseball from a small ball game to a long ball game. He hit 659 homers for the New York Yankees and is most famous for his time with the Bronx Bombers in the 1920s and early 1930s. Ruth dominates the list of Yankee home runs hitters, as he is 123 ahead of Mickey Mantle, who is second on the

list. However, the Babe started his career with the Boston Red Sox and hit his first three home runs *against* the Yankees. These four-baggers were swatted in 1915.

3. MOST HOME RUNS, ALL FOR ONE TEAM

Many people who are asked about the slugger with the most home runs in a career with all of them hit for the same team answer Mickey Mantle with 536 for the Yankees. However, Hall of Famer Mike Schmidt played his entire career with the Philadelphia Phillies and hit 548 circuit clouts, the most of any player.

4. MOST CAREER HOME RUNS WITHOUT HITTING A GRAND SLAM

The batter who hit the most career homers without ever hitting a grand slam is Glenn Davis with 190 dingers. Davis played ten big league seasons with the Houston Astros and Baltimore Orioles from 1984 through 1993. He had 66 career at bats with the bases loaded, collecting 13 hits and 44 RBIs in those situations. He hit four doubles and one triple but never cleared the fence. All of his batting numbers with the sacks full were well below any other game situation for him in his career.

5. BOUNCE HOME RUNS

Before 1931, any ball that landed in fair territory and bounced out of play was a home run under the rules of the day. There are more than 700 documented examples of bounce home runs before the rule was changed to the modern equivalent, which is that such hits are doubles. A frequently asked question regarding bounce homers is how many Babe Ruth hit. The answer is that he never hit a bounce home run, although his teammate, Lou Gehrig, hit two.

6. DON MATTINGLY'S GRAND SLAMS

During the 1987 season, Don Mattingly hit six grand slams, which broke the old record of five in one year held by Ernie Banks (1955) and Jim Gentile (1961). The curious part of this performance by Donny Baseball is that he never hit another in his 14-year career.

7. PINCH ME

On May 24, 1947, manager Ben Chapman of the Phillies started a right-handed pitcher against the Brooklyn Dodgers at Ebbets Field. This was nothing more than subterfuge, as he intended to replace the hurler with one who threw left-handed almost immediately. Al Jurisich faced two batters, getting one out in the process, before Chapman brought Oscar Judd to the mound. Judd added one base runner and recorded one out before Dodger skipper Burt Shotton sent righty Carl Furillo to pinch-hit for lefty Gene Hermanski. Chapman's tactic failed, though, because Furillo blasted the first pitch he saw for a three-run home run, which propelled the Dodgers to a 4-3 victory. This is the only time a batter has hit a pinch home run in the first inning of a game in major league history.

8. RUTH LAPS THE PACK

Babe Ruth hit his last three homers on May 25, 1935, as a member of the Boston Braves. They were hit at Pittsburgh's Forbes Field, and Ruth played his last game five days later. On May 25, Ruth was the career home run leader with 714. His former teammate, Lou Gehrig, was second with 352 dingers. Thus, when Ruth retired, he had more than twice as many home runs as anyone else in history. In fact, Rogers Hornsby was the only other player with 300 that day.

q. MOST HOMERS WITHOUT WINNING A SEASON TITLE

Rafael Palmeiro hit 569 home runs in his career playing for the Cubs, Rangers, and Orioles, but never led his league in homers for a season. The closest Raffy got was in 1999, when he hit 47 dingers and finished second to Ken Griffey, Jr., who hit 48 that season. Palmeiro's 569 homers are the most for any hitter who never led the league for a season.

10. FIRST AT BAT HOMER

Gary Gaetti is one of about 100 players who have hit a home run in his first major league at bat. Gaetti doubled up on that feat by also hitting a home run in his first post-season at bat. He is the only player in history to do this in both regular season and post-season.

Sing a Song of Four-Baggers

There have been many songs through the years that use baseball as the main topic, or at least mention the sport in the lyrics. Some of these songs refer to home runs in one way or another. Here are some of my favorite examples of homers in song.

1. "KNOCK IT OUT OF THE PARK"

Sam and Dave recorded this song in 1970 and The Nighthawks also recorded the tune in 1998. The title obviously refers to a home run but there are also a number of lyrics that mention four-baggers. In the chorus, the singer tells the listener: "When you hit the ball, knock it out of the park." There are a number of comparisons between baseball and love in the song. For example, "Love is just like a baseball game, I've been told before. You don't win by getting on base, you gotta make a score." And: "All of your kisses have got to have that spark. And when you're fooling around, you have to knock it out of the park."

2. "THAT LAST HOME RUN"

In 1974, McKinley Mitchell and Willie Dixie recorded a song inspired by Hank Aaron's 715th homer. "Hank was going some when he hit that last home run." As they say in the song: "The homer was heard all over the world."

3. "MOVE OVER BABE (HERE COMES HENRY)"

Bill Slayback, who pitched for the Detroit Tigers from 1972 through 1974, wrote this song, with long-time Tigers broadcaster Ernie Harwell, in 1973. Later, Slayback recorded the tune. Part of the chorus says: "Hank's hit another, he'll break that 714." Perhaps the best line in the song is: "When The Hammer hits one out, that's what baseball is all about."

4. "DID YOU SEE JACKIE ROBINSON HIT THAT BALL?"

In 1949, Count Basie and his band recorded this tune, which talks about Robinson hitting homers and stealing bases. This was a good year for the song to debut, as Robinson was named the National League Most Valuable Player in 1949. This swinging number talks about the ball "zooming towards the left field wall."

5. "LOVE IS LIKE A BASEBALL GAME"

This is another song that compares love and baseball, as they say that "three strikes and you're out." The Intruders recorded the tune in 1968 and it reached number 26 on the pop charts. The best line in the song is: "I thought I hit a love run." There are probably many players who thought that through the years.

6. "CENTERFIELD"

John Fogerty's hit song contains the refrain "Put me in coach, I'm ready to play—today." However, the key line for us is "Just hit the ball and touch them all." Early in the song, the Fogerty lyric is strangely reminiscent of a 1959 song that is listed as number nine below: "Just roundin' third and headin' for home, it's a brown-eyed handsome man."

7. "D-O-D-G-E-R-S SONG (OH, REALLY? NO, O'MALLEY)"

Danny Kaye released this recording in 1962. Both Kaye and the Dodgers had moved from Brooklyn to Los Angeles to further their careers. The song relates a "game" between the Dodgers and the San Francisco Giants. In the top of the first "Orlando Cepeda, with a wham, bam, he hit a grand slam." Then: "top of the fifth, Say Hey Willie Mays hits a three-bagger down the right field line, but he's out trying to stretch it to a homer as Roseboro tags him on the bottom of the spine." Kaye later was part owner of the Seattle Mariners.

8. "CHEAP SEATS"

The country group Alabama recorded this song in 1993. It talks about people at a minor league park in "the cheap seats" who talk a great game but have little clue about what is going on. Lines such as "We've got a great pitcher, what's-his-name" really tell the story here. The fans also say: "We don't worry about the pennant much, we just like to see the boys hit it deep." At the end of the recording there is a homer call by a "broadcaster."

9. "BROWN EYED HANDSOME MAN"

Rock & Roll Hall of Famer Chuck Berry's 1957 song, "Brown Eyed Handsome Man," mentions a ballplayer in one of the verses. Although Berry got the ball and strike count backwards, the lyric is classic Berry: "2-3 the count with nobody on, He hit a high fly into the stands, He rounded third, he was headed for home, It was a brown eyed handsome man."

10. "A DYING CUB FAN'S LAST REQUEST"

We have saved the best home run song reference for last. This 1981 tune by Steve Goodman, who wrote the hit song "The City of New Orleans," talks about the last request of a

Cubs fan who never got to see the team win a pennant. This funny song talks about the fan's request for a funeral at Wrigley Field. He says: "When my last remains go flying over the left field wall, we'll bid the bleacher bums adieu and I'll come to my final resting place out on Waveland Avenue." Goodman died in 1984, just a few days before the Cubs clinched the National League East title.

The Ten Craziest Questions Jayson Stark Has Ever Asked Me

Jayson Stark probably has asked me more questions about home runs than any other person on the planet. Many of them have been pretty crazy and most of them have been enlightening. He has written a column called "Useless Information Department" for many years, first with the *Philadelphia Inquirer* and now with ESPN. Here is a sample of the best questions he has asked.

1. BACK-TO-BACK AND DO IT AGAIN

In 1992, Jayson first contacted me to ask about a feat performed by Gary Sheffield and Fred McGriff of the San Diego Padres. On August 6 of that year, they hit back-to-back homers in the first inning and then again in the second inning. This concept seemed unique at the time but we discovered a fairly long list of players who had previously done this.

2. I CANNOT COUNT THAT HIGH!

On September 25, 1998, Detroit Tigers teammates Juan Encarnacion and Frank Catalanotto hit back-to-back home runs in the third inning of a game in Toronto. Jayson's question: Is this the longest combined length of last names to hit back-to-back jacks? Indeed, it was. Their combined length of

22 letters beat out three pairs of sluggers who had 21 letters in their last names, the most recent of which was Carl Yastrzemski and Rico Petrocelli in 1974. Encarnacion and Catalanotto repeated their feat on August 6, 1999. A pair of Braves sluggers tied this mark on June 5, 2007, as Jarrod Saltalamacchia and Chris Woodward hit consecutive homers against the Marlins. Saltalamacchia's 14-letter last name is the longest in history—why don't we just call him "Salty"?

3. THANKS, DAD!

Only three players have hit a home run off a team managed by their dad. On June 19, 2002, Bret Boone homered for the Seattle Mariners in an Interleague game against the Cincinnati Reds, managed at the time by Bob Boone. David Bell hit a home run for the Mariners against the Colorado Rockies, managed by Buddy Bell on June 14, 2001. Moises Alou is the undisputed champion on this question, however. While playing for the Houston Astros, Moises homered off the Montreal Expos four times from 1998 to 2001 while his dad, Felipe, managed the Expos. Then in 2003 and 2004, Moises, now with the Chicago Cubs, hit five home runs against his dad's San Francisco Giants. Thus, Moises has homered for two different teams off two different teams managed by Felipe.

4. BUT I LIKE IT HERE!

In 2000, Magglio Ordonez of the Chicago White Sox hit 18 consecutive home runs in the state of Illinois. The blasts occurred from June 24 through September 29. One might think this is nothing special—he hit 18 in a row at home, right? Wrong! On July 8 and 9, the Sox played the Cubs across town at Wrigley Field and Ordonez smacked one homer each day. This oddity resulted in a search for the longest such streaks in one state. Two players made great use of favorable ballparks to hit 25 consecutive four-baggers at home. In 1884, Fred Pfeffer of the Chicago White Stockings (now Cubs) hit all 25 of his home runs at Lake Front Park, which had the shortest fences of any major league park in history. Then in 1932, Chuck Klein of the Philadelphia Phillies hit 25 in a row in Pennsylvania. From June 6 through the end of the season, Klein hit three at Forbes Field in Pittsburgh and 22 at Baker Bowl in Philadelphia.

5. EITHER SIDE, IT DOESN'T MATTER

In 2003, pitcher Carlos Zambrano of the Chicago Cubs hit two home runs—one hitting right handed and one hitting left handed. This, of course, generated a question about other hurlers who have performed this feat. Tony Mullane (1887), Kid Nichols (1898 and 1901), Bill Donovan (1901), Garland Buckeye (1925), Early Wynn (1953), Cal McLish (1957), Jerry Walker (1962), Jim Perry (1968), and Joaquin Andujar (1979) had all done this. Zambrano repeated the feat in 2006 and 2008, making him the switch-hitting slugging pitcher champion.

6. YOU HAVE HOW MANY?

A few years ago, a pitcher had surrendered a lot of homers early in the season and was threatening to give up more gopher balls than homers hit by the top batter that season. This has actually happened a few times in history. Most of them were before the start of the Lively Ball Era in 1920, but two hurlers have accomplished this feat in the last few decades. In 1974, Mickey Lolich of the Detroit Tigers gave up 38 home runs to lead the majors in that category while Mike Schmidt of the Philadelphia Phillies hit *only* 36. Then in 1986, Bert

Blyleven of the Minnesota Twins surrendered 50 home runs, the most of any pitcher in one season in history. That season, Jesse Barfield of the Toronto Blue Jays hit 40 blasts to lead all sluggers.

7. DIDN'T YOU JUST HIT ONE?

On May 6, 1995, Jerome Walton of the Cincinnati Reds hit a two-run home run in the bottom of the ninth inning to beat the New York Mets, 13-11. The next day, Walton led off the bottom of the first inning with another four-bagger. Thus he ended a game with a homer and started the next one with a homer. Six other batters had done that before: Joe Gordon of the Yankees in 1940, Dick McAuliffe of the Tigers in 1965, Tony Gonzalez of the Phillies in 1967, Lou Whitaker of the Tigers in 1987, Mariano Duncan of the Reds in 1989, and Roberto Kelly of the Yankees in 1990. Scott Hairston of the Padres repeated the feat in 2007.

8. MULTI-HOMER GAMES IN THE SERIES

In the 2002 World Series, Tim Salmon of the Angels hit two home runs in one World Series game but he had not had a multi-homer game all season before that! We found 12 guys who had done that before Salmon: Chad Curtis of the 1999 Yankees, Dave Henderson of the 1989 Athletics, Alan Trammel of the 1984 Tigers, Willie McGee of the 1982 Cardinals, Davey Lopes of the 1978 Dodgers, Tony Perez of the 1975 Reds, Gene Tenace of the 1972 Athletics, Tony Kubek of the 1957 Yankees, Charlie Keller of the 1939 Yankees, Benny Kauff of the 1917 New York Giants, Harry Hooper of the 1915 Red Sox, and Patsy Dougherty of the Red Sox in the first World Series in 1903.

9. **MORE HOMERS THAN WINS**

In 2003, Brooks Kieschnick of the Milwaukee Brewers, who had been an outfielder, tried pitching on a regular basis. He also found himself in the lineup many days as the designated hitter. Kieschnick hit seven home runs that season while compiling a 1-1 record as a pitcher. He homered as a pitcher, designated hitter, and pinch hitter and hit more home runs than he collected wins as a hurler. Surprisingly, Vladimir Nunez of the Florida Marlins had also performed this feat by hitting one home run and winning no games during the 2000 season. The last pitcher to do this before Nunez had been Dave Eiland in 1992, who hit one home run for the Padres while winning no games.

10. **OH, BROTHER!**

It is rare for a pitcher to face a hitter who also happens to be his brother. From 2000 through 2004, Tim Drew pitched in the major leagues while his older brother, J.D., also played in the majors. Although they never faced each other, Jayson naturally asked about brothers hitting home runs off brothers. This has only happened three times in history. George Stovall of the Indians, who hit 15 homers in his career, hit his first on October 7, 1904, off his brother, Jesse, who pitched for the Tigers. Rick Ferrell of the Red Sox homered off Indians pitcher Wes on July 19, 1933. They had formerly been teammates. Joe Niekro, a pitcher for the Houston Astros, hit his only career homer off his brother, Phil, on May 29, 1976.

It's a Most Unusual Day

There have been more than 250,000 home runs hit in major league history. Most of those are credited when the batter hits a fly ball over an outfield fence. However, baseball can provide unusual moments of many types, including home runs that don't seem to fit the profile. One such unusual play occurred on August 14, 1901, at New York's Polo Grounds. The Boston Beaneaters were playing a doubleheader against the Giants and, in the second game, player/manager George Davis of the Giants hit the ball down the left field line. There were two New York policemen standing in the corner of the field talking and, before they could get out of the way, the ball struck one of them on the shoulder and bounced into the bleachers. Umpire Bob Emslie ruled it a home run over the protests of the Boston squad. This is a result of the rule before 1931 that said a ball that bounced in fair territory and out of play was a homer. Here is a sample of some of the most unusual home runs ever recorded—and, yes, these things actually happened in a major league baseball game.

1. RUN BUTTED IN

On May 26, 1993, in a game at Cleveland Stadium, Indians designated hitter Carlos Martinez hit a fly ball to deep right field to lead off the bottom of the fourth inning. Jose Canseco, patrolling right field for the Rangers, chased down the ball. At the last second, he turned his head to look for the fence, the ball flew past his glove, bounced off his head, and flew over the wall. The scoring on the play? A home run for Martinez and a "run butted in" for Canseco. The Indians, behind 3-1 at the time of the homer, rallied to win the game, 7-6.

2. THE PINE TAR SPECIAL

On July 24, 1983, one of the strangest dramas ever involving a home run played out at Yankee Stadium in New York. With two out in the top of the ninth inning, George Brett of the Kansas City Royals hit a two-run homer off Goose Gossage to give the Royals a 5-4 lead. While Brett sat in the dugout after running the circuit, New York skipper Billy Martin protested that the bat was illegal and the umpires, after consultation, called Brett out for having pine tar on his bat higher than is allowed by the rules. Thus the score reverted back to 4-3 and the game was over, with the Yankees as the winners. Brett was ejected along with three other Royals. On July 28, American League President Lee McPhail overruled the umpires when he upheld the protest of the Royals. Because of McPhail's decision, the game's situation reverted to a 5-4 Royals lead with two out in the top of the ninth inning and had to be completed on August 18. Thus, Brett hit a home run, which became an out minutes later, and then was turned back into a homer four days after the fact!

3. IF IT AIN'T BROKE, OR EVEN IF IT IS

On May 28, 1981, Steve Henderson of the Cubs singled to center field in the fourth inning of a game at Wrigley Field.

Shortly after that, Pirates catcher Tony Pena picked him off first base and while diving back to the bag, Henderson broke his right hand. In the fifth inning, he homered to left field with one man on, two men out, and one broken hand. He was out of action until August due to the fracture. Henderson hit five homers that season and 68 in his career.

4. PUT IT *On* THE SCOREBOARD—YES!

The visiting Cincinnati Reds beat the Brooklyn Dodgers, 7-2, on June 22, 1936, at Ebbets Field. In the fifth inning, Ival Goodman hit a fly ball to right field that landed on top of the scoreboard and remained there. The ball was still in play but it did not come down to the field so that the outfielders could retrieve it. Rather, it sat on the ledge at the top of the scoreboard. Meanwhile, Goodman raced around the bases for a very unusual inside-the-park home run. This is an example of the run *really* being put on the board.

5. PUT IT *In* THE SCOREBOARD—YES!

Two remarkably similar freak home runs were hit at Boston's Braves Field at the end of the Deadball Era. At the time there was a ground-level scoreboard in left-center field, which had a three-column lineup area with each player listed by a number. The number for the player currently at bat would be slid into the center column leaving a twelve by six inch hole in the board at his lineup spot. In the first game of two on July 11, 1919, Cincinnati Reds catcher Bill Rariden, a former Brave, hit a ball that bounced a couple of times and headed for the scoreboard. Rariden's hit hopped into the hole at his slot in the lineup. The young man running the scoreboard was looking through the hole at the game and the ball nearly struck him before he could move out of the way. This tied the score at two each and the Reds eventually won in extra innings, 4-2. Johnny Rawlings repeated the feat on August 14, 1920. Rawlings's hit came in the seventh inning of the second game that day while playing for the Philadelphia Phillies (to whom the Braves sold him that June). This time the ball went through a spot in the lineup board where the hole was half open, the number being partly in two different columns. The solo shot put the visitors ahead, 3-2, but the Braves won the game in ten innings, 4-3.

6. HELLO, WHO'S THERE?

At Shibe Park in Philadelphia, the Washington Senators beat the Athletics, 15-7, on April 18, 1932, with a 15-hit attack that included three homers. The Nats scored six runs in the top of the ninth inning to put the game out of reach. Sam West smacked a three-run blast and Joe Judge a two-run shot, both off Jimmie DeShong. The ball that Judge hit for his first home run of the season went over the right field fence and crashed through the window of a house overlooking the ballpark. To the amusement of those in the park, a woman came out of the house to see what had caused the crash.

7. GET UP, GET UP, GET OUTTA HERE! IT'S GONE!

On May 6, 1916, Brooklyn's George Cutshaw hit a trick home run at Ebbets Field in the eleventh inning. The hit fell into right field near the wall and looked to be a double for the batter. However, the ball slowly rolled up the fence and over the top into the street, thus becoming a game-ending homer. According to the *New York Times* story, "Instead of receiving the plaudits from 20,000 spectators, which ordinarily would follow a winning home run in the eleventh inning of a hard-fought battle, the Dodger second baseman crossed the plate amid a storm of laughter, which eventually turned into meek applause."

8. THE KICK IS UP . . . AND IT'S GOOD!

On June 14, 1916, the Brooklyn Robins (now Los Angeles Dodgers) hosted the St. Louis Cardinals at Ebbets Field. Bruno Betzel led off the top of the fourth inning and hit a line drive to left field. Zach Wheat moved toward the line to field the ball and accidentally kicked it into the bleachers. Under the rules of the day, it was a home run for Betzel.

9. HE REALLY NAILED THAT ONE

Cardinals third baseman Les Bell hit a solo homer in the fourth inning against the New York (now San Francisco) Giants on July 25, 1926. The ball looked like it was going into the right field stands at Sportsman's Park in St. Louis but it struck a projection on the wall and dropped toward the playing field. The ball seemed to hang suspended above right fielder Ross Youngs, who tugged at the ball while Bell ran the circuit for an inside-the-park homer. Youngs failed to get the ball because it was stuck on a nail in the wall!

10. HOME RUN SECURITY SYSTEM

On August 22, 1886, the Louisville Colonels hosted the Cincinnati Reds. As was frequently the case in the 19th century, the home team batted first in this contest. In the top of the eleventh inning, William Van Winkle "Chicken" Wolf hit the ball past center fielder Abner Powell. As Powell chased after the sphere, a small dog caught him by the leg and held him several seconds. Meanwhile, Wolf ran the circuit for an inside-the-park home run.

Mr. Gopher Ball

Fans love home runs. Batters love home runs. Pitchers, however, do not. In the history of Major League Baseball, only ten hurlers have surrendered 400 four-baggers. To give up that many, you have to be a good pitcher who plays for many years in the majors—below average pitchers do not get the opportunity to pitch that long. Here are the all-time leaders in gopher balls surrendered.

1. ROBIN ROBERTS, 505
Robin Roberts pitched for 19 seasons in the majors for four teams. He is the only pitcher to surrender 500 homers. Duke Snider hit 19 off Roberts, the most by one batter off one hurler. Roberts won 286 games, struck out 2,357 batters, was selected for five All Star Games and was elected to the Hall of Fame in 1976. Oh, by the way, he hit five home runs in the big leagues. In 1956, Roberts surrendered 46 four-baggers, which was the single-season record for 30 years (see Bert Blyleven below for the current mark).

2. FERGIE JENKINS, 484
Ontario native Fergie Jenkins pitched for four teams in 19 years. He won the National League Cy Young Award in 1971

and pitched in two All Star Games. Jenkins hit 13 homers, won 284 games, struck out 3,192 batters in his career, and was elected to the Hall of Fame in 1991.

3. PHIL NIEKRO, 482
Knuckleballer Phil Niekro pitched 24 years in the majors for four teams. He struck out 3,342 hitters while winning 318 games. Niekro pitched in two All Star Games and was elected to the Hall of Fame in 1997. One of the 482 homers was hit by his brother, Joe—Joe's only career home run. Phil hit seven four-baggers.

4. DON SUTTON, 472
Don Sutton ranks fourth on the list of homers surrendered with 472. He pitched 23 years in the majors and holds many pitching records for the Dodgers. His career record includes 324 wins, 3,574 strikeouts, and four All Star appearances, including being named the All Star Most Valuable Player in 1977. He was elected to the Hall of Fame in 1998. Sutton, a below-average hitter, never hit a home run but did start his career with a five-game hit streak in which he collected seven singles.

5. JAMIE MOYER, 464
Jamie Moyer has pitched 22 years in the majors for seven teams through 2008. He has 246 wins and 2,248 strikeouts during that time. He surrendered 44 homers in 2004 to lead the American League while pitching for the Seattle Mariners, which is the fifth-highest single-season total in history.

6. FRANK TANANA, 448
Frank Tanana pitched for 21 years in the majors for six teams. He led the American League in strikeouts in 1975 with 269 and finished his career with 2,773 punch outs. He won 240 games and pitched in one All Star Game.

7. **WARREN SPAHN, 434**

Warren Spahn is one of the few players memorialized in a poem. In the late 1940s, Braves fans used to think: "Spahn and [Johnny] Sain and pray for rain," which is a reference to a poem printed in the *Boston Post* in 1948. Spahn pitched 21 years for three teams, including seven times in the All Star Game. He won 363 games and struck out 2,583 batters. Spahn hit 35 homers, second on the all-time list for pitchers. He won the Cy Young Award in 1957, and was elected to the Hall of Fame in 1973.

8. **BERT BLYLEVEN, 430**

Bert Blyleven was born in the Netherlands and pitched 22 years for five teams. He struck out 3,701 batters while winning 287 games. Blyleven led the American League in complete games (24) and strikeouts (206) in 1985. In 1986, he surrendered 50 home runs to set the single-season record.

9. **STEVE CARLTON, 414**

Steve "Lefty" Carlton pitched for six teams in 24 years, primarily for the Cardinals and Phillies. He struck out 4,136 batters while winning 329 games. Carlton led the league in strikeouts five times and in wins four times. He pitched in five All Star Games, won four Cy Young Awards, and was elected to the Hall of Fame in 1994. Carlton hit 13 homers in his career.

10. **DAVID WELLS, 407**

David Wells pitched 21 years in the majors for nine teams. He won 239 games and struck out 2,201 hitters in that time. Wells pitched in three All Star Games and was selected as the American League Championship Series MVP in 1998.

Clash of the Titans

The odds of two players with a combined total of more than 1,000 home runs playing in the same game are very small. And since sluggers cannot simply hit a homer any time they wish, the odds of seeing both of them hit a home run in the same game are *really* small. In fact, this has only happened 33 times in history. Here is the list of times when two sluggers with the most combined homers each hit one in the same contest. All these instances are by players on opposing teams. The top total for teammates in one game is 1,052 by Barry Bonds (734) and Moises Alou (318) of the Giants on September 23, 2006.

1. HANK AARON AND WILLIE MAYS

For the only time in history, two batters with 600 homers each both hit one in the same game. On May 8, 1971, the Atlanta Braves played the Giants at Candlestick Park in San Francisco. Willie Mays hit the 634th homer of his career in the sixth inning and Hank Aaron followed with his 604th in the eighth frame. They had combined for 1,238 home runs—the largest total in history for any two batters who homered in the same game.

2. BARRY BONDS AND MANNY RAMIREZ

On June 17, 2007, Barry Bonds of the San Francisco Giants hit his first career home run at Boston's Fenway Park. It was the 748th of Bonds career and came in the sixth inning of the 9-5 Red Sox victory. One inning later, Boston's Manny Ramirez hit his 480th career homer. Thus, the two sluggers had combined for 1,228 home runs at that point.

3. BARRY BONDS AND RAFAEL PALMEIRO

In the first game of two on June 12, 2004, the Giants played an 11 inning game at Baltimore and won, 9–6. In the top of the third, Barry Bonds hit his 675th home run to score the first run of the contest. Then in the bottom of the frame, the Orioles scored three times, including two on a homer by Rafael Palmeiro. Raffy hit another four-bagger in the eighth inning and ended the day with 537 career blasts. Bonds and Palmeiro combined for 1,212 home runs, the third highest total of all time.

4. HANK AARON AND BILLY WILLIAMS

On June 19, 1976, Hank Aaron, in his last season as a player, joined his Milwaukee Brewers teammates in Oakland to play the Athletics. In the sixth inning, Aaron hit career homer number 751 in a losing cause. In the seventh inning, Oakland's Billy Williams plated the last run of the game with a home run as the Athletics beat the Brewers, 7–4. It was homer number 422 for Williams, so the combined total in this game was 1,173.

5. HANK AARON AND WILLIE McCOVEY

San Diego was the scene of this encounter on August 6, 1974. Hank Aaron of the Braves plated the first three runs of the contest with his third inning blast. It was career homer number 728 for Aaron. In the bottom of the ninth, the Padres scored their only two runs when Willie McCovey hit his 428th home run. Aaron and McCovey had combined for 1,156 four-baggers that day.

6. HANK AARON AND BILLY WILLIAMS
Aaron and Williams appear together on this list twice. This instance happened on June 12, 1975 in Milwaukee. Hank led off the bottom of the fifth with a homer, number 739 in his career. Billy hit his in the eighth inning with two on and two out; it was his 400th career blast. Williams was the 16th player to reach the 400-homer milestone and he and Aaron combined for 1,139 dingers that day.

7. WILLIE MAYS AND ERNIE BANKS
On June 17, 1970, the Cubs invaded Candlestick Park in San Francisco to play the Giants. In the top of the eighth inning, Ernie Banks hit his seventh of the season and 504th of his career. In the bottom of the frame, Willie Mays provided the only run of the game for the Giants with his 15th homer of the season and 615th of his career. This was the first time in history that two sluggers with at least 500 homers each both homered in the same game. Their combined total at the time was 1,119 home runs.

8. SAMMY SOSA AND JIM THOME
A pair of designated hitters provided the fireworks in Arlington, Texas, on August 30, 2007. In the top of the first inning, Jim Thome of the White Sox hit a home run that provided the only run of the contest for his team. In the bottom of the second, Sammy Sosa started the scoring for the Rangers with his own solo shot. Those were the only two four-baggers in the 5–1 Texas victory. The dinger was number 606 for Sosa,

while Thome climbed closer to the 500 Home Run Club with number 495; thus they combined for 1,101 circuit clouts through that day.

9. SAMMY SOSA AND KEN GRIFFEY, JR.

Sammy Sosa and Ken Griffey, Jr. each homered in the same game on June 12, 2005 as the Orioles played the Reds in Cincinnati. Sosa hit two that day, in the second and third innings while Junior hit a two-run homer in the fifth inning. This was the fourth time and most recent time that two players with 500 homers each both homered in the same contest. Sosa (582) and Griffey (512) ended the day with 1,094 combined home runs.

10. BARRY BONDS AND CARLOS DELGADO

On April 26, 2006, in San Francisco, the Mets beat the Giants, 9–7, with two runs in the 11th inning. In the bottom of the ninth, pinch hitter Barry Bonds hit a three-run homer to tie the score at seven each. It was Bonds' 711th career homer and the fourth pinch-hit blast for him. Carlos Delgado had hit a four-bagger in the third inning for the Mets, which was his 378th home run. The two sluggers combined for 1,089 career dingers.

Forever Young*

O ne of the data items tracked for each major league player is the date of his debut in the big leagues. The seemingly trivial date is useful in tracking a player's performance in many statistical categories but when paired with a player's birth date, it can create some unusual combinations. The following nine pitchers surrendered home runs to batters who were born *after* the pitcher made his major league debut. To qualify for this list, a pitcher had to have been very good at his job in order to pitch that long in the majors. This is the asterisked list in the book, as there are only nine entries. Congratulations on finding it!

1. HERB PENNOCK
Hall of Famer Herb Pennock started his career on May 14, 1912, and played until 1934. On September 23, 1933, Pennock surrendered a home run to Mel Almada, who had made his debut 15 days earlier. Almada was born on February 7, 1913, nine months after Pennock pitched his first game in the majors. Then, on May 25, 1934, Pennock surrendered a homer to Hal Trosky, who had been born on November 11, 1912. Pennock was the first pitcher to qualify for this list and he performed the feat with two different batters.

2. EARLY WYNN

Early Wynn made his big league debut on September 13, 1939, and played through the 1963 season. On August 21, 1962, Wynn surrendered a four-bagger to Boog Powell, who had been born on August 17, 1941, almost two years after Wynn's debut. Then, on September 28, 1962, Wynn surrendered a bomb to Joe Pepitone, who was born on October 9, 1940. Wynn was elected to the Hall of Fame in 1972.

3. WARREN SPAHN

Hall of Fame pitcher Warren Spahn pitched his first big league game on April 19, 1942, but joined the Army in 1943, returning to baseball in 1946. Spahn surrendered a home run on June 21, 1964, to Rusty Staub, who was born on April 1, 1944 (two years after Spahn's debut). In 1965, Spahn surrendered two homers to batters born after his debut. First, Tony Perez took Spahn deep on April 30 and then Alex Johnson repeated the feat on August 31. Perez was born on May 14, 1942, while Johnson was born on December 7, 1942.

4. PHIL NIEKRO

Phil Niekro, who was elected to the Hall of Fame in 1997, made his major league debut on April 15, 1964, and spent most of his career with the Braves. On July 13, 1986, Niekro surrendered a home run to Ruben Sierra, who was born on October 6, 1965. Jose Canseco, born on July 2, 1964, homered off Niekro on September 13, 1986.

5. TOMMY JOHN

Tommy John might be most famous for a surgical procedure named after him, but he pitched 26 years in the majors and appeared in two All Star Games. John made his debut on

September 6, 1963. On May 31, 1987, Mark McGwire, born October 1, 1963, homered twice in one game off John and then on July 5, 1988, Ruben Sierra, born October 6, 1965, homered off John. Sierra, who had already hit one off Phil Niekro in 1986, was born more than two years after Tommy John's major league debut.

6. NOLAN RYAN
Hall of Fame pitcher Nolan Ryan debuted on September 11, 1966, and pitched for 27 years in the majors. Four different batters who homered off Ryan qualify for this list. The first was Ken Griffey, Jr., who was born on November 21, 1969, more than three years after Ryan's debut. Griffey homered off Ryan on June 22 and September 19, 1990. Carlos Baerga, born on November 4, 1968, homered off Ryan on April 26, 1991. Travis Fryman, born on March 25, 1969, took Ryan out on July 28, 1991. Finally, Kevin Koslofski, born on September 24, 1966, homered off Ryan on August 27, 1992.

7. CHARLIE HOUGH
Honolulu native Charlie Hough made his major league pitching debut on August 12, 1970, and his last appearance on July 26, 1994. He played for the Dodgers, Rangers, and White Sox, and started the first game in the history of the Florida Marlins in 1993. On May 26, 1992, Ivan Rodriguez of the Rangers hit a home run off the knuckleball pitcher, who was hurling for the White Sox at the time. Rodriguez was born on November 27, 1971.

8. MIKE MORGAN
Mike Morgan, who made his debut on June 11, 1978, pitched for 12 different teams in a career that lasted until 2002. On

Knuckleballer Charlie Hough pitches for the Chicago White Sox.
Ron Vesely/Chicago White Sox

June 22, 2002, Vernon Wells, who was born on December 8, 1978, hit a home run off Morgan in an Interleague contest. Morgan only pitched in two more big league games after this day.

q. **ROGER CLEMENS**

Roger Clemens made his debut on May 15, 1984, with the Red Sox. On June 21, 2007, rookie Troy Tulowitzki of the Rockies, who was born on October 10, 1984, homered off Clemens, who had recently signed a contract with the Yankees and was making his third start of the season. Then on August 18, 2007, a youngster took Clemens deep for the second time in the same season as rookie Cameron Maybin of the Tigers hit a solo homer the day after his debut. Maybin was born on April 4, 1987, almost three years after Clemens pitched his first big league game.

Index

The Author

David Vincent is a long-time member of the Society for American Baseball Research (SABR) and was presented with the organization's highest honor, the Bob Davids Award, in 1999. Vincent graduated from the University of Massachusetts, earned a Doctor of Musical Arts degree from the University of Miami, and is a computer systems engineer for EDS.

He is referred to as "The Sultan of Swat Stats" by ESPN and is regularly consulted by Major League Baseball, ESPN, FOX, *USA Today*, and many other media entities on the history of the home run.

Vincent is the author of *Home Run: The Definitive History of Baseball's Ultimate Weapon*, co-author of the award-winning book, *The Midsummer Classic: The Complete History of Baseball's All-Star Game,* and *SABR presents the Home Run Encyclopedia. Parade* magazine ran a feature on Vincent in 2005 and *USA Today* ran one in 2007.

He is the founding secretary of Retrosheet and regularly lends his expertise to this and other baseball history websites. Vincent has been an official scorer in four minor leagues and is now official scorer for Major League Baseball in Washington, D.C.

He and his wife, JoLynne, live in Northern Virginia.